Kill Me Not

Peter N Muya

Published by Peter N Muya.

Kill Me Not

Peter N Muya

Published by Peter N Muya, 2024.

KILL ME NOT

Peter N Muya

First edition. July 2024.

Second edition. May 2025

Copyright © 2025 Peter N Muya.

ISBN 9798227961501

For information contact Bishop Peter Muya via muyabishop@gmail.com or via phone +254724805868/+254798649468

Edited by Peter Hinga Kiago. Email: quibpet3r@gmail.com phone +254706488565

Also by Peter N Muya

Love Without Lust
Do Not Weep
Death From Illicit Brew
Hope For Survival
I Shall Not Die
Never Lose Hope

DEDICATION

Let me dedicate this book to the youth especially, pupils in schools and students in colleges. I have started a campaign dubbed, I Shall Not Die, to rescue them from drug abuse and alcoholism.

"Kill Me Not!" I cried. "You women, sellers of the illicit brew, drug dealers, drug peddlers... I will never be a slave of your poisonous stuff!"
BISHOP PETER N. MUYA.

Foreword

IN THIS BOOK, BISHOP Muya's faithfully explains biblically how young people are perishing in drug addiction and alcoholism. He believes that they can be rescued by helping them to discern evil behaviors after reading the word of God them.

How I wish this book could land in the hands of every pastor, church member and the community. This is a story of redemption from drug abuse, in a series of self- harm.

There is a great need for the world to know the gospel which can help them to recognize how evil behaviors are destroying our children and youth in this evil times. This important book is written at the right moment, when the drug abuse menace is a problem that definitely should be addressed.

It is our highest time as believers of the word of God to re-define our mission and vision so as to go out to rescue our young people before they die prematurely in drug abuse. We are to go out to make them hear the truth from God's word which is able to set them free from all types of addiction. They desperately need to hear from us the good news about their deliverance from evil behaviors.

The bible says, if the son of God sets you free you shall be free indeed. Bishop Muya is going around the country trying to rescue the youth from drug-related problems. As the war from evil behaviors rages, many victims are to be rescued before they perish. Bishop Muya loves the youth and that's why his mission is to make sure they are redeemed from addiction. I too love them and that's why I joyfully recommended this book as a memoir of redemption from evil behaviors which are destroying our youth.

You shall know the truth and you will be set free from drug abuse.

Apostle Stephen Kimono.

IN MY LIFE I DID NOT experience comfort or fatherly love during my childhood, because both parents were perpetual drunkards. They were impoverished living in a mud and grass thatched hut given to them by their employee- the white settler in those days.

We eventually, had to make illegal homemade alcohol to make money to survive. At home we were given the illicit brew by our parents free of charge. We had a craving for more drinks in our blood as we became teenagers.

We lived a reckless time of trial and error, and in those times drug abuse left us with scars that we carried into adulthood. We suffered physical, mental and emotional damage.

When I became an adult, I tried filling the empty void in my soul with drinks, drugs, pleasure and fornication. But still, I felt empty and hopeless. These mood altering substances caused complications in my stomach. I needed medical treatment, but I ignored it. My life needed an overhaul. I was enslaved by destructive drugs. They had induced artificial feelings of hopelessness. Many were the times I thought of committing suicide.

Drugs created exhilaration, which caused illusions, hallucinations, anxiety and brief reverie of joy. I was also, addicted to pornographic obsessions. These evil images robbed me of my self-respect, freedom, self-control and peace of mind

I was always high and had no regard for God or religion. I had woes, sorrows, contentions and complaints. My eyes were always red and I had wounds in my soul, body as I experienced hell on earth. This was my dilemma. I could not see a way out.

When I was tired of living in addictions, I cried "Kill Me Not! You women, sellers of the illicit brews, drug dealers, drug peddles. I will never be a slave of your poisonous stuff again!"

The time came when I realized that I was a sinner in the deepest hell. I called Jesus Christ to save me from sins, addictions and evil behaviors. Jesus came into my heart and cleansed me with his precious blood. I became a living testimony in the ghettos, villages and slums. I started witnessing to my friends, relatives and neighbors. I joined Full Gospel Church in Kiambogo village.

Today I'm a pastor who is busy rescuing the youths and communities from drug abuse and illicit brew consumption. Join me in my campaign against this threatening menace dubbed "I Shall Not

Die!"

Read this book, Kill Me Not, and I'm sure you will experience salvation, deliverance and healing from drug abuse or alcoholism. I will also help you on how you can consult Doctors or how you can join a rehabilitation Center like "Christ Ordained Kids Organization" a registered [CBO] Under the ministry of labor and social protection, based in Nakuru town. We are in a rehabilitation business, rescuing the street children from all kinds of sexual or drug abuse.

Acknowledgement

I WANT TO THANK MR. Mburu for typing my manuscript and Peter Hinga for editing this book. Also let me thank the leaders of "Stay Up Rehabilitative Community Based Organization" for their moral support.

Chapter 1

MY DILEMMA

I SPUTTERED INTO THIS troubled and painful world. Thank God I was safely born. I came out from the darkness of my mother's womb and saw the light of day for the first time. The Bible tells me that "I was born in iniquity and in sin did my mother conceive me" (Psalm 51-5). I was born like any other human being: naked and empty-handed.

The village women celebrated my birth with great joy. They shouted at the top of their voices five times to announce that a baby boy had been born in the house of Muya, in accordance with the Kikuyu customs. Mother wrapped me with old rags and put me in a bed made with sticks.

My parents were impoverished. They were living in a mud-and-grass-thatched hut given to them by their employers—the white settlers in those days. During the rainy season, Mother would repair our hut's leaky roof. I did not experience comfort or fatherly love in our home during my childhood. My father was a perpetual drunkard, and he seemed to have a grudge against me. At a very young age, I experienced child abuse. I can remember my father beating me many times after school for no reason. The beatings became worse as I started growing up.

I loved my father; despite the bad things he was doing to me. *What is wrong with me?* I'd wonder. In school, teachers were proud of my classroom achievements, and they'd say I was doing well overall. My classmates loved me very much. My father used to withhold my school tuition fees sometimes, but he would pay my brothers' or sisters' fees on time. Many times, I was sent home from school to bring the school fees back. It humiliated me.

When my mother would ask my father why he was mistreating me, he would insult her publicly. He would curse me by saying I would not make it in life. Mother encouraged me, but my father was a significant barrier in my life. I was a very bright boy. And I made it through, even though my father didn't want to give me any moral support.

Father was very harsh on me. He would throw my report form when I gave it to him and then condemn me in front of family members. I used to go to a solitary place behind the school compound repeatedly and cry for hours, wondering when this abuse would end.

Sometimes all hell would break loose between Dad and Mum because of me. But when my mother went to the market, and I was alone with my father, I would pay for it. Father would beat me when my mother was not around. He would beat and chase me at night, without giving me any supper. Mother would send my brothers to bring supper to me. My sisters knew about this grudge, so they sided with me.

My sisters would signal me to run away before Father would have a chance to catch me. He also mistreated others at home. Sometimes Mother would intervene and defend me. She used to give all of us children her undivided attention to make up for

Father's abuse. I often wondered why my father carried all that hatred towards me.

As a parent, do you love all of your children without discrimination? Remember. Your children are gifts from God. In school, as well as in the village, I used to be a disciplined young man. Many parents in the village admired my good character traits and attributes.

Mother always had a smile on her face after looking at my report forms. The teachers in school wanted to be associated with me. At home, however, we were all enduring hardships. We learned to live a simple life with little means. We endured, and not because we wanted to, but because that was the only way.

My mother tried her best to keep us from the evil influence of some of the villagers. Father used to live recklessly, and he could not afford to buy us a plot for our own house. We lived in the village without hope. Mother encouraged us to study so we could purchase plots for our parents and for ourselves.

I was encouraged by my mother to attend Sunday service in a nearby Catholic church. As children, we were taught to memorize verses of scripture—I related to the story of Joseph in the Bible. I learned how he was mistreated by his brothers and how, eventually, God promoted him. This story helped me to endure the abuse and the beatings from my father.

We eventually had to make illegal homemade alcohol to make money to survive. At home, we were given the illicit brew by our parents, free of charge. We had a craving for more drinks in our blood as we became teenagers. We lived a reckless time of trial and error, and these times left us with scars that we carried into adulthood. We suffered physical, mental, and emotional damage.

When I became an adult, I tried filling the empty void in my soul with drinks, drugs, pleasure, and sexual immorality. But still, I felt empty and hopeless. Little did I know that I was lost and slipping into the deepest pit of hell daily. Every day I was going further down the drain.

My family became involved in many evil behaviors to survive. I hated this harmful way of life. I was addicted to drugs, alcohol, and sexual immorality. I kept company with a bad young man. The Bible says, "Bad company corrupts good morals/habits" (Corinthians 15:33).

My brother and I were caught by police many times because of the crimes we would commit in the village. Our mother paid our fines in court so that we would be released. I would swear that I would never be involved in drugs or alcohol consumption again, yet I would eventually suddenly become hooked again. I was a slave to the evil powers of the devil.

Our relatives and the villagers knew we were drug addicts, so they feared us. These mood-altering substances caused complications in my body, and especially in my stomach. I needed medical treatment, but I ignored it. My life needed an overhaul.

Can my behavior be changed? I wondered. I was enslaved by the destructive drugs. They had induced artificial feelings of hopelessness. Many were the times I thought of committing suicide.

Drugs created exhilaration, which caused illusions, hallucinations, anxiety, and brief reverie or joy. I was also addicted to pornographic obsessions. These evil images robbed me of my self-respect, freedom, self-control, and peace of mind. My heart always felt guilty and dirty. I felt empty and unfulfilled by my life. I was fighting with my age-mates because of girls in the village. I was trapped in many kinds of evil behaviors.

I drowned my problems with more drugs and alcohol. I was always high and had no regard for God or religion. Despite all of my problems, my mother made me attain good grades in school.

We lived together with our father in the same house, but he had abandoned all fatherly responsibilities. I was in mental turbulence and thought I could never find a solution to my problems. I was in a terrible situation. The hand of the devil had gripped our whole family. The villagers branded me as "The Drug Addict." It was a nickname that accurately described my situation.

I had woes, sorrows, contentions, and complaints. My eyes were always red because of my drug abuse. The serpent called "drugs" bit me hard. I had deep wounds in my soul and body as I experienced hell on earth. This was my dilemma. I could see no way out.

In school, due to the hard life I was being brought up in, I wanted to study and become a preacher like John the Baptist in the Bible. But when I left school, the devil made sure that I could not pursue my dream of becoming a preacher. I wanted to be a preacher so that I may help my family come out of drugs and alcohol. Instead, my life was so hard that I eventually became very bitter towards God and anything concerning religion.

I asked questions like, "Why was I born?" and "If God lives, then why has He allowed us to go through these evils in our family?" Why were these evils following me from my childhood? Early in my childhood, I thought my father disciplined me as his child because I was disobedient. Yet still, as I grew older, the beatings only increased. I could not understand why he always heaped abuses on me in front of the whole family.

Sometimes, Father used to call me in when he was on a drunken spree and tell me that I'm his "Muthoniwa" (in-law), referring to my maternal grandfather after whom I was named. He didn't even call me his son. "Please buy me a bottle of beer or two, Muthoniwa," Father told me, but I declined. I had qualms about obeying his orders. I joined the whole family in trying to help Father stop his drinking, but it was all in vain. Eventually, he reconciled himself to the fact that at his age of over seventy years, there was no further harm to be done to his body if he continued drinking.

Even though Father was very violent under the influence of alcohol, we still respected him. He would never regret what he had done the previous day. He cherished his evil habit of drinking very much. *How can we get Dad out of this addiction?* the whole family wondered. But when my brother, David, and I become teenagers, we joined my father in the drinking dens.

I remember that in my hey-days, I would go around from den to den drinking as well as sleeping with anything that wore a skirt. Thank God that in those days, there was nothing like HIV/AIDS. I'd always manage to go home without the virus and without a penny in my pocket. Sometimes I woke up locked in a police cell, having been caught in the drinking dens unconscious.

I started drinking at the tender age of thirteen. As a teenager, I was spoiled by alcohol and sex. I was young and very stupid. Many times, after waking up in the morning, I could remember my evil behaviors of sleeping with ugly, older women.

I started thinking of ways to recover from addiction and sexual immorality. I had dreams of marrying the one girl whom I could honor and respect as my only wife and leaving ugly women to die in the drinking dens. I vowed that after marriage; I would never break our marital vows. But an hour later, I would hear the footsteps of my friends coming to collect me to go for a free drink, after which I'd find myself tempted and falling into the bottle again.

I am writing this story to warn my friends, children, and grandsons never to drink or abuse drugs. Drug addiction and alcoholism disheartened me, and that's why I have decided to help addicts to be set free in my campaign against drug abuse and alcoholism. I call my program, "I shall not die."

I am targeting young boys and girls between seven and thirty-five years of age. This is the age range when many young boys experiment with drugs, ignoring the fact that it could lead them to a situation where it'd be almost impossible to treat their addictions. I urge parents to help their children to recover from addictions.

I would not want you to go through the evils that I had experienced in my life. I will never forget how Mother used to give me a glass of chang'aa when I came home from school, instead of giving me lunch. After letting me sleep on the floor of our house on an empty stomach, she would then tell me to go out and sell the illicit brew to her customers. When I woke up, my father subjected me to all sorts of curses, and he said that I was against him just as my grandfather was. He hated me because I was named after my grandfather. He also envied the big coffee farm my grandfather owned in Kiambu County.

I cannot forget when I would come home from school with classmates and my father would embarrass me in front of my friends and even in the presence of any other visitors we may have had at home. Sometimes he would throw me out in the cold and command me to go to sleep without eating supper. However, Mother always spared a plate of food and sent my brothers to bring it to me outside.

I was one of his biological sons, but why did he continually mistreat me for nothing? Sometimes I would wonder if I was born out of wedlock. When I remembered his abuses, especially when I was drunk, I would become very bitter towards my father.

One day I remember saying in my small hut, "Enough is enough!" I was thinking of surrendering my life to God, but this thought did not last. The devil tightened his grip on me. I believed I was born under a curse. I tried to study specific family patterns and acquired our family history from the beginning.

In the town, I would meet some of my classmates driving big cars, while others would have big businesses. I wondered what was wrong with me. Although I did well in school, after school I was a failure in life and wallowed in a sea of evil addictions. I was involved in all sorts of evils with extreme enthusiasm.

I was badly off financially, so I would go to my friends to beg for a drink and a puff of drugs. But, the effect of my drug abuse was devastating. Sometimes I found myself sweating, and my heart would race much more than usual. In the illicit brew dens, I was a star whenever I had the money to buy my friends drinks. Drinking made me think that I was escaping from my problems. Unfortunately, when I would wake up in the morning, I'd have the same issues, if not more, not to mention the hangovers I experienced in the morning.

Every morning I went into my mother's house to take tea. She tried to nurse me by telling me to stop my evil behaviors, but after only a few hours, she would hear me shouting in the drinking dens.

My soul had a vacuum that I was trying to fill with drugs, illicit brew, and sexual immorality. I always suffered when I tried to withdraw from my drugs. Drug abuse is destroying our youth in schools, in colleges, in towns, and in rural areas.

As I abused a few rolls each day, my body was becoming steadily weaker. I started losing memory and experiencing fearful nightmares and dreams.

I`m writing this to warn the youth because many are being destroyed by drug abuse. Many young people who have dropped out of school have engaged themselves in crimes, such as rape and snatching purses or wallets in the streets to get money for drugs. While some are stealing, others are committing suicide.

One day I started to regret the years I had wasted in drugs and alcoholism. I decided to quit from the illegal ways of life and dehumanizing habits. However, let me tell you openly that with drug addiction, it is only God who can deliver you from this evil habit.

Drugs had ruined my life and stolen my joy and peace of mind.

One roll was purchased for a pound in those days. I was using two to three rolls a day and was always high. Many times, I was collected sleeping by the roadside by the villagers. Other times I was found sleeping on the floor of "Mama Pima's" house after drinking chang'aa in her home.

My life was at a crossroads, and I was hoping to find a way out. I was lonely. Nobody in the village wanted me to share my woes and problems with them since they had their own share of problems.

I wanted to come out of my evil life. I thought drinking would help solve my problems, but it didn't. Drugs brought no joy to my troubled life. Instead of blaming myself for my problems, I blamed others. I started experiencing seizures and feared that I might have been developing a mental disorder. I wanted to quit from evil and all those behaviors. Sleep was the only luxury I could afford because it was free of charge. Many days when I went home drunk, I slept with an empty stomach. Most nights were deadly experiences, for I had nothing to eat.

In the morning, instead of going to seek tea, I would wake up searching for the illicit brand with an empty stomach. Because of how I indulged in drinking, my age mates nicknamed me "Mukundi," which means "a perpetual drunkard" in my dialect.

Deep in my soul, I was yearning for liberty from all those severe addictions. *But, how could I get out?* I would wonder.

Drugs had damaging consequences in my life. My health became very bad. I was faced with a life-and-death decision, but the pain of withdrawal made it feel as though I was going to die anyway. I opted to continue with my lifestyle because whenever I tried to withdraw, I experienced agonizing pain in my body. Addiction was a part of my life, so to part with these addictive forces meant death.

Drugs could make me forget my problems, but only for a moment. I wanted to end my life. There was a feeling that the dead were happier than I was. I wanted to die and meet the happy guys in hell. I could not sleep at night when I thought about my problems and misfortunes. I felt as if nobody loved me or understood me. I felt as if everybody in the world was against me. I was experiencing hell and felt that God had abandoned me. The world treated me with injustice. I was tired of living in this world of unrest. I thought that one day I would rest in my soul.

Every day, from sunrise to sunset, my problems accumulated. Those were the darkest days of my life. Every morning I woke up hoping for the best but found the opposite. I remembered the day I missed death by a whisker.

Whenever I read a local newspaper, I would go straight to the pages of the dead, the obituary page, and look at the images of the guys whom I thought had overcome the world through death. I wanted to be like them, but the question I asked myself was, "Where would I spend eternity?" I felt that the latter world would be better than the former. I used to crack jokes with my age-mates by telling them that I wanted to die and meet many of my friends in hell.

I wanted to die because I was confused, disappointed, and frustrated. Little did I know that I was the devil's project. I couldn't differentiate fact from fiction. This was my dilemma. *Who will rescue me from my dilemma?* I wondered every day.

Chapter 2

I SURVIVED DEATH FROM DRUG ABUSE

With so many frustrations, I started thinking deeply about my miserable life as I painted the chilling picture of perpetual drunkard parents. Being brought up in a threatening environment, I was trapped in the web of illicit alcohol and drug abuse. Together with my brothers and sisters, we went to school with the hope of making our lives better for the future. However, everything seemed barbed and dangerous after we finished schooling.

In the village, we did not enjoy the fruits of education, for we were always high and hopeless. Poverty is unjust; it enslaved us. *Who will help us to alleviate this anguish in our family?* I wondered. The illicit brew and drug abuse was breaking my family. In my soul, I heard a sobering voice that stirred me to make the decision to change my life once and for all.

"Kill Me Not!" I cried. "You women, sellers of the illicit brew, drug dealers, drug peddlers... I will never be a slave of your poisonous stuff!" I was born and brought up in this crooked generation. I was born in the kingdom of darkness. I was a slave of sin in the kingdom of Satan. But now, I am a new person. My sins simply separated me from God.

The time came when I realized that I was a sinner walking in the deepest hell. I called Jesus Christ to save me from my sins. Jesus came into my heart and cleansed me with His precious blood. I was made completely a new creation. The Bible encouraged me, "Therefore, anyone in Christ Jesus is a new creation; the old has gone, the new has come" (2 Corinthians 5:17).

After my salvation, the pastor in charge of my local church organized a water baptism service for all those who were saved the following Sunday. The pastor said that Jesus had commanded his disciples to be baptized by immersion. He quoted, "Therefore, go and make disciples of all nations, baptizing them in the name of the Father and of the Son and of the Holy Spirit" (Matthew 28:18–19).

We were taught what water baptizing is all about. We were made to understand the key to obtaining a victorious and liberated Christian life. I understood the term "baptized" as meaning to be "totally immersed in water." After proper teaching, we were taken to the river some kilometers from the local church for a Sunday service. When the service started, we were baptized one by one in water. To me, this personal thing is the act of going under the water and rising up from the grasp of a demon.

The consumption of alcohol is as old as mankind. It is a custom that has been related to all African communities. Although legally accepted, alcohol has the potential to cause harm to the consumer if abused. Traditionally, alcohol consumption was restricted to the elders of the community. It was also present in forums to exchange views, conclude communities' agreements, resolve disputes, formalize marriages, etc.

Historically, most of the African communities consumed fermented alcoholic drinks, which had less alcoholic content than the illicit brews and alcoholic beverages of today. Sadly, alcoholic consumption has lost its traditional values because it has been commercialized. Teenage drinking has gained more prominence. The introduction of the second-generation brews and other brews has worsened the situation. Therefore, the country has witnessed widespread consumption of alcohol, especially among the youth.

The survey conducted by the "National campaign against drug abuse authority a few years ago indicated that 13% of Kenyans who are between the ages of fifteen and forty years consume alcohol. It also revealed that most abused alcoholic drinks are the second-generation brews, which are mostly packaged in plastic bottles or in sachets and sold to anybody, including very young boys.

All these illicit brews are causing premature deaths, blindness, impotence, and other health complications to the consumers. The misuse or abuse of alcohol in the country has resulted in severe social-economic consequences such as widespread domestic violence, increased road accidents, reduced economic production, school attendance, and HIV transmission.

Substance abuse is emerging as a serious security challenge. Kenya has been serving as a transit point for narcotic drugs from other countries involved in drug trafficking. These drugs include heroin, mandrax, blaze, and cannabis. I was addicted to cannabis. It is also known as "bhang," and it is locally cultivated around Lake Victoria, Kisii, Central Highlands, Mt. Kenya, and along the coast, as well as imported from Uganda and Tanzania.

As a drug addict, I was a perpetrator of sexual offenses and other crimes. Assault was the most serious offense that was inflicted on women and girls. I was a perpetrator when I was under the influence of drugs and alcohol. Domestic violence was very high in our village because of low incomes and low literacy levels. I was suffering without hope from unemployment, lawlessness, and poverty.

I was worshiping evil powers that I did not even know of. alcohol and drugs were my gods. I was living a failed life of hopelessness. I had a trembling body and a languishing heart. The Bible described my life accurately: "who has woes," "who has sorrow," "who has strife," "who has complaints," "who has wounds without cause," and "who has redness of eyes" are all "those who go to try mixed wine."

"Do not look at wine when it is red when it sparkles in the cup and goes down smoothly. In the end, it bites like a serpent and stings like an adder. Your eyes will see strange things. You will be like one who lies down in the midst of the sea; or like one who lies on the top of a mast. 'They struck me,' you will say, 'but I was not hurt. They beat me, but I did not feel it. When shall I wake up? I must have another drink'" (Proverbs 23:29–35).

I was a wishful thinker. In the morning, I wished it was evening, and in the evening, I wished it was midnight. The horror of dreams of death was disturbing me at night. I was drinking to escape these fearful dreams. The evil dreams made me very frustrated and confused. I lived as though I was cursed. I felt I was cursed in the village and cursed in the city.

Everywhere I went, I saw signs of death because of my moral decay. In the village, life was a horror, a proverb, and a disaster. The devil had continually oppressed and tormented me. I was living in hell on earth. The devil was against me, my family, and the villagers.

There were many times I was collected by my sisters as I slept on the roadside drainage ditch after being high. One day in a drunken stupor in Lanet Center, nine kilometers from Nakuru Town, I was riding my bicycle on the highway towards home when I was hit from the back by a speeding lorry. My right hand got broken, but I survived death by a whisker. I was rushed to the Nakuru Hospital by a good Samaritan. But when I recovered, I continued drinking.

My elder brother, David, was also a drug addict. In a drinking spree, he assaulted a group of gangsters. He was almost beaten to death. He was rushed to Nyahururu Hospital. When the doctors noticed that he had two compound fractures in both legs, he was placed in a cast for three months.

Alcohol was responsible for more admissions to hospitals than any other single cause. Together with my brother, we used to be arrested by the police on several occasions and taken to the cells because of alcohol-related crimes. Alcohol caused my father's death. It caused injuries in our bodies, left our lives broken, fractured our bones, and caused misery and agony in our family.

The drinking and selling of alcohol by my mother brought misery, violence, and wickedness to our family. There was no peace at home.

When the village Christians visited us at home to comfort us following many tragedies and incidents, my brother, David, accepted Jesus Christ as his personal savior. He was saved and delivered, and changed completely.

One year later, after observing my brother's changed life, I also accepted Jesus Christ as my personal savior. I was delivered from death to eternal life. I was changed from a crooked generation to a chosen one. Suddenly, no more drugs or alcohol and no more sexual immorality.

I found my brother in the Full Gospel Church in the Kiambogo Village, Gilgil. My brother became a teacher in the same village, and a few years later, I became a full-time pastor in the village church. Today, I am a presiding Bishop in the Gospel

Messengers Church in East and Central Africa. My ministry is changing the lives of people who had been living as slaves of sin, bondage, and addiction.

The youth and many families are being tormented and suffering from evil habits and addictions. I am pointing them to my redeemer and savior, Jesus Christ, who has the power to save and heal their lives and bodies. I'm telling victims that the best treatments total abstinence from alcohol and drugs and by accepting Jesus Christ as your personal savior. Jesus has all the answers to your problems.

I go around the country telling people how God's redeeming love arrested me after I accepted Jesus Christ as my personal savior. Today, I am a new creature. I am a blessed child of God. God singled me, selected me, and bestowed his favor upon me. I was given the privilege to be God's own property. I am now saved eternally by the blood of Jesus Christ. I'm wholly hidden in Jesus Christ.

I'm a living testimony in this hurting world. God's grace and power are making me go out to speak to drug addicts and alcoholics. Before God, I am a vessel of honor in His kingdom. God is releasing his incredible anointing in my ministry. When I stand in the open-air meetings to preach the gospel to sinners, people say that "surely God saves."

I preach the gospel, and at the end of every meeting, I break the spirit of alcoholism. Many people give their lives to Jesus Christ. God called me to break all the altars of alcohol, smash all idols, and burn them with fire. I'm called by God to follow and emulate Jesus Christ. I am blessed and don't care whether people love me or not. I don't care whether my neighbors love me or not. When the neighbors whisper to me that I will not make it, I raise up my voice high and shout aloud, "Hallelujah!"

I know that with Jesus Christ behind me, I will make it no matter what! Every day there is an inner voice that says, "Go and preach the gospel." I will make it. That's why I walk my testimony, live my testimony, and embrace my testimony. I was dead, and now I am alive. I was delivered from death by Jesus Christ, my savior.

John 5:21 says, "For as the Father raises the dead and gives them life, so also the Son gives life to whom He wills." Verse 24 is clearer: "Truly, truly, I say to you: whoever hears my word and believes Him who sent me has eternal life. He does not come into judgment but has passed from death to life."

That's why I preach the gospel confidently I have crossed over from death into life eternal. In these end times, I'm raising my voice very high to call people from death to life eternal. I will speak of the goodness of God boldly in this hurting world. I had been changed from a drug addict into a preacher of the gospel.

I am in the world, but I am not of the world. I am a chosen generation. That's why the world hates me. I'm a citizen of heaven. I'm a chosen vessel. I am not a cheap vessel made of cheap materials like plastic. I'm made of pure gold. I'm God's treasured possession. I am a chosen vessel that cost God His begotten son. I'm appointed, consecrated, and set apart for divine purposes. I am an ambassador of God. I was bought with a price: the blood of Jesus Christ.

Drug abuse and alcoholism are causing a lot of domestic violence, murder, divorce, and suicide cases. That's why, as a former drug addict, I'm conducting the most prominent campaign against drug abuse dubbed, "I shall not die." This campaign is derived from the word of God in Psalm 118:17, "I shall not die but live and declare the works of God."

Recently in our village of Kiambogo, villagers, leaders, and the media witnessed a woman who was weeping helplessly because of her children. They had quarreled with her husband because of a glass of milk. The husband was a drug addict in the village. The man demonstrated his anger by holding his young child and knocking him against a stone. Instantly, the child died. The mother had run away, and the other child had escaped with serious injuries. The man was to be tried for murder.

In this book, you will be reading cutting-edge stories on counseling and rehabilitation for drug addicts and alcoholics using biblical based, gospel-centered ways of recovery, rehabilitation, and restoration.

I'm teaching pastors in our local churches comprehensive messages on how to help victims from different kinds of addictions. I am always called in the village to solve cases of domestic violence and conflict in the families. I am helping many with personal and emotional needs. Many victims are delivered from depression, stress, hopelessness, and poverty. They are living sober lives in the church.

Although I am carrying out my mandate to preach the gospel in the country, drug abuse has emerged as a major social challenge and threat to national peace and security. The youth are most of whom are affected, posing a serious threat to the productivity of the working-age group in the country.

The youth tend to engage in crimes as a way of raising funds to sustain their drug-dependent style. We have organized criminal gangs with different names who are operating secretly in villages, towns, cities, and throughout the whole country.

I wish to reiterate that the fight against drug abuse and the consumption of illicit brews is a joint venture that must be handled through teamwork and partnership of the government, nongovernmental organizations (NGOs), and the church.

The government, in its wisdom, enacted the "Alcoholic Drinks Control Act 2010" in an attempt to bring sanity to the alcoholic sector. The objective of the law was to protect the health of the consumers from excessive consumption of alcoholic drinks as well as promote treatment and rehabilitation programs for addicts. However, the problem of alcoholism is beyond the legal approach alone because it is affecting everybody. It is a social problem.

That's why, as a pastor and a former addict, I am very much concerned about this hurting issue. I am doing an outreach campaign against alcohol consumption and drug abuse. I am conducting public education and sensitization programs on the harmful effects of alcohol and drug abuse right from the villages up to the national level.

Our treatment and rehabilitation of addicts should be instituted as a matter of national priority. Together, with all stakeholders, we are going to bring sanity to the alcoholic sector as we give healing and transformation to the addicted.

In my campaign, I read from the Bible, "There is death in the pot" (2 Kings 4:38–41). My message to the victims is to embrace sobriety and avoid the poison from the pot of the illicit brews. That's why in my life and ministry, I declare that "I shall not die." I will live to preach the gospel in this hurting world.

That's why I say, like Apostle Paul, that "I have been crucified with Christ. It is no longer I who live, but Christ lives in me, and the life which I live now in the flesh, I live by faith in the Son of God, who loves me and gave himself for me" (Galatians 2:20). I was a drug addict, but I cried, "Heal me, Lord, and I shall be healed.

Save me, and I shall be saved, for you are my praise" (Jeremiah 14:17).

Thousands of villagers are poor because of their wrong choices in life. One of these choices is to abuse drugs and alcohol. Many men in the villages refuse to work but instead go from house to house looking for the dangerous brew. Alcohol addiction and idleness are the leading causes of poverty in rural areas. Many families are living in turmoil because many husbands are running away from their responsibilities at home.

I have declared a life-and-death battle against drug abuse in the villages and the slums where men meet in the drinking dens to drown their stress and problems with alcohol. Criminal activities are rampant in these areas. In the villages, estates, and slums, where they sell and consume alcohol and abuse drugs, the crime rate is very high. People involve themselves in violence, rape, assault, and prostitution. Women and girls have terrible stories to tell. People live in fear because of criminals.

When I first visited the slum dwellers, I was surprised to see that many were families sleeping on the floor with very cheap mattresses or with some tattered bedding, which were packed together in one corner of the house after use. Another terrible thing in the slum area is that human waste can be seen openly in every empty space. So, during the day, the smell of the waste becomes very strong and a very dangerous health hazard.

All these conditions are caused by poverty, alcoholism, and hopelessness. Many families consider a child as a burden because they are very poor. That's why many children in these areas end up in the streets and young girls become prostitutes. We have many cases of abortion as well.

This is why I preach the gospel in these areas. I have a long-term solution. I am encouraging former addicts in my church to start income-generating projects so that they cannot be hooked by their evil behaviors again.

Chapter 3

SET FREE FROM ADDICTIONS

IN THIS EVIL-FILLED world, I was a wreck in life. My life was in chaos, for I apparently chose to indulge myself in sex abuse, drug abuse, and alcohol addictions. I was thinking about committing suicide. The thought of ending my life was hanging in my mind. However, I did not know that after death, I would be eternally separated from God. I did not know that my life was like a vapor and that one day I would vanish forever. I did not know that after death, I would be ushered by the angels before the holy God, and thereafter be dashed into the deepest parts of hell to be tormented by the devil forever.

I was in the kingdom of the devil and bound in sin, and addictions. I was moving hopelessly with the wrong group of friends. I was pushed by lust and pleasures. Because of drug abuse, I was suffering from social problems, regrets, disillusions, and hangovers. I was equally suffering physically, emotionally, and mentally. I was blind before I realized that I needed somebody to save me from sins, bondage, and addictions.

That's why I decided to call Jesus Christ into my troubled heart. He came in and washed me with His precious blood. I was saved, healed, and delivered. I was set free from addictions. Since that wonderful day, I never again drank wine, puffed any drug, or slept with a woman or a girl except for my wife. God helped me have a very successful wedding in the church. Today I am a full-time pastor, and that's why I am teaching the youth the dangers and consequences of abusing drugs.

Jesus is helping me and answering the many questions that I've had in my rotten life. I joined the church, where I grew up spiritually and was taught how to serve others and preach the gospel. I enjoy winning souls for Christ. I love preaching the gospel to all. However, I focus on drug addicts and alcoholics.

I've taught the word of God in the church and preached the gospel in the open-air meetings. Friends, neighbors, and relatives gave their lives to Jesus Christ, and they were set free from sins, bondage, and addictions. Even now I preach Christ on the cross. I know preaching of the cross is foolishness to those who are lost, but it is power to those who receive Christ as their personal savior.

I teach the word of God to the youth in schools and in colleges. I'm rescuing the youth before they perish in drug abuse and alcoholism. My campaign against drug abuse is dubbed, "I shall not die, but I will live and declare the works of God" (Psalm 118:17). I am conducting healing and deliverance services for the youth who have behavioral manifestation and those who are suffering from devastating problems related to dependence on drug abuse. Drug addiction and alcohol addiction are diseases.

As a former drug addict, God has given me the grace to eradicate drug abuse completely in our society. I don't treat symptoms, but I go deep into the root cause of craving and addiction. I feel concern for those who fall victim to them. Many of my members in the church are former addicts who became totally delivered. I tell victims that Jesus has the power to save, heal, and deliver addicts from abuse.

The Bible says, "If it is the son of man who will set you free, you shall be free indeed" (John 8:36). Are you a drug addict or sex pervert? I have good news for you; Jesus can set you free from any type of addiction.

Drugs are destroying our youths in schools and colleges. When students abuse drugs, it interferes with their perceptions and moods, and many of them fail examinations. Drugs have both psychological and physiological effects on a student's body. Many students abuse drugs to withdraw from reality. Students are a soft target of drug peddlers. They'd say they experience sexual arousal, wakefulness, a lessening of fatigue, or an increase in energy and self-confidence.

The beginners start with either a puff or two pills or a sip of illicit brew. Then, after experiencing the psychological effects of the drug, they come to want more and more. This becomes an addiction. Once a victim is hooked on drugs, he or she will keep increasing the dose. Students cherish drugs so that they can stay in a wild state. Many student addicts will organize strikes and demonstrations in schools. These students may also commit suicide.

There are those hard drugs that are made from flowers, stems, leaves, and seeds, e.g., bhang. The types of drugs obtained from plants are marijuana and hashish. Marijuana is derived from the dried leaves and the stems of the plant, while hashish is obtained from the resin found covering the flowers of the female plant.

The strength of the drug is usually related to the geographical area where the plant was grown. The effects of bhang may be noticed after twenty-five minutes. The effects of this drug for the experienced user include daydreaming, speaking freely, and getting pleasurable relaxation. At first, the user may become dizzy or start to vomit, but let me say that the effects of all these drugs seem to be related to one abuser's personality and the environment that the abuser is used to.

In other words, bhang exaggerates personality as well as group identity. The effects of bhang are therefore closer to those of alcohol than those of drugs. It also causes impairment in both intellectual and psycho-motor activities, especially in those who are not experienced users of the drugs.

Many drugs have psychological effects, including false peace in the abuser's body. They bring a sense of illusion rather than reality. The victim gets emotional problems, which can cause him or her to commit suicide. It may be fifteen minutes after abusing the drug before the effects appear. Some drugs are odorless, tasteless, colorless, or mixed with sugary liquids either for deliberate abuse or for someone who is not used to them. When the drug is abused for a long time, psycho-dependence on the drug can occur. Many students consider themselves heroes after taking drugs. Drugs cause disobedience and rebellion to the students.

Another drug called heroin is made from opium. The main effect of this drug is that it slows down both mental and physical activities. It also causes sexual apathy. It increases the craving for more drugs. It creates a feeling of temporary relief from tensions.

A person who is high on this drug has the symptoms of small pupils, a dreamy look, slurred speech, drowsiness, and an aversion to noise. When the abuser becomes sober, the symptoms include irritability, as in the abuser wants to be alone and may perspire. After the abuser has used the drugs continuously for some time, he or she becomes dependent on it, and it takes time for the abuser to return to normal.

When the abuser becomes addicted, he or she becomes a slave to drug and will fight with anybody to get the drugs even if it means committing a crime. Today, drug abuse is experienced in many nations of the world, including on our beloved continent of Africa.

In schools and colleges, I can say that drugs interfere with perception and with studies. The student therefore, regardless of his or her potential, will start getting poor grades, and eventually, he or she will become a dropout. The student will become a problem in school, at home, and in society.

That's why, as a gospel minister, I'm starting a ministry to go into schools and colleges to preach the gospels of Jesus Christ. I'm doing pastoral counseling in schools and colleges and rescuing many youths from drug abuse and addiction. I know there is a gradual treatment that is given by doctors to the victims of drug abuse. Still, though, I'm giving total deliverance from drug abuse by using the Bible, as well as Jesus Christ, who has the power to deliver sinners from sins, bondage, and addictions. Jesus sets the drug addicts free instantly, and they become

transformed. The world is fighting drug abuse, and I am joining in that fight.

Many people who are found to be in possession of drugs must be arrested and charged in court. The fight against drug abuse is recognized internationally. Students and other young people are looking to us to rescue them. We are working very hard with school heads to end the drug abuse menace in schools.

We have many willing ministers of the gospel ready to help in the fight against drug abuse. Many of the former addicts tell us that they had tried everything but could not be delivered. After surrendering their lives to Jesus Christ, they become totally delivered and set free from addictions.

In our ministry office, we are always available. You can share your problems with addiction with us. We are willing to share with you all information on how to be delivered from drug abuse. Call us or email us, and we shall respond soon. We are teaming with NGOs that the country governments had established to put an end to this menace.

Before I was delivered, my life was a mess. I was suffering from many problems and life pressures. It was as if I was in a pressure cooker boiling with difficulties. I had developed regular headaches, ulcers, nausea, heart problems, high blood pressure, and a host of other evil ills that are linked to drug addiction.

When I was unable to cope with all these pleasures in life, I started searching for a cure and deliverance. That's when I was led to Jesus Christ, who delivered me completely. I laid to Him all of my problems, burdens, bondage, sins, and addictions. I was healed and transformed. My parent's family members and neighbors saw a great change in my life.

The power of the word of God is now shining in my new life. I went into the church and participated in all spiritual services and functions. Every day I grew spiritually. I had no choice but to serve my God as I witnessed how the power of God in Jesus Christ transformed me.

I can tell you boldly that Jesus Christ is the Lion of Judah who prevailed in my life. I am unable to restrain tears of joy from welling in my eyes when I remember how I was changed and transformed. I thank God for that change. Jesus carried away my burdens, sorrows, grief, pressures, evils, sufferings, illnesses, and iniquities on His cross. I was born again. I was changed from a crooked generation into a chosen generation in the kingdom of God. The power of God had transformed me gradually, spiritually, and socially.

That's why I am telling the youth that Jesus is the answer in your life today. Without Him in your life, you will be lost in hell after dying in your sins. Call Jesus Christ now in your life, and you will experience a new life. Jesus knows your name and all the problems you are going through. Let Him save you now, for He has invited, "Come to me all who labor and are heavily laden, and I will give you rest" (Matthew 11:28).

Chapter 4

KILL ME NOT

MY LIFE WAS MISERABLE due to my addiction to drugs and alcohol. I felt that there was no sense in me living in this evil world any longer. I started cursing my parents bitterly for bringing me into this world. I displayed my bitterness openly by abusing drugs.

In my desperate condition, no solution was forthcoming. "All my intimate friends detest me; those I love are turned against me. I am nothing but skin and bones" (Job 19:19–20).

Therefore, I hated life, and the thought of committing suicide flashed in my mind. Every day I was pushing myself deeper and deeper to hell with my sins. Fortunately, however, the time came when I began searching for an unknown thing that would relieve my tortured soul. I had tried everything that could be offered but there seemed to be no hope of finding a successful cure for my miserable condition.

All of my friends were those who the Bible describes as the ones who wanted to drink anything that is bitter. "Woe to those who rise early in the morning to run after drinks, who stay up late at night till they are inflamed with wine" (Isaiah 5:11).

It was during these dark days when liquor was controlling my aching body and my enslaved mind. I was a complete wreck and a social misfit. All of my friends and family members feared me and wanted to desert me. I was engulfed in anguish and despair.

"If only my anguish could be weighed and all my misery placed on the scale, it would surely outweigh the sand of the sea" (Job 4:2–3). *Should I commit suicide?* I wondered. I remembered one incident that involved one of my friends and I said I could not do that kind of foolishness.

I shed tears as I thought about my family and how they had sacrificed themselves in our lives of hardships. I thought about my mother and how she was risking her life doing the illegal business of brewing the illicit brew known as "chang'aa" at night and escaping the police dragnet. This outlawed business was the lifeline of our poor family's income. My brothers and sisters were also willing participants of this illegal business and even other worse money-making ventures, all in the name of survival.

How will I come out and also pull my family out of this miserable way of survival? I pondered. The only way to stop such a business, one that we relied on in order to survive, was to make the life of our poor family uncertain. When I was crying for my life, and that of my family, I found a book at home written by Billy Graham that explained to me how to be born again.

As I read page by page, the reality that I was a sinner according to the word of God became very real. My heart felt as if Jesus Christ was knocking on my door waiting for me to welcome Him. "Behold. I stand at the door and knock" (Revelation 3:19).

One day I was drunk and high as I rode my bicycle home from a drinking spree. I heard a loud *bang* when I was hit from behind by a speeding lorry. I was left by the roadside weeping in a pool of blood and seriously injured. But I survived death by a whisker, for God had protected me. Fortunately, a good Samaritan took me to Nakuru General Hospital, and the doctors worked very quickly to save me. However, the medical report showed that the abuse of alcohol had destroyed brain cells and put me at risk of a stroke or heart attack. The bad thing was that after I was discharged from the hospital, I still continued drinking and abusing drugs. At home, the police were searching for the assailant of a girl.

My desperation and hopelessness caused me to attempt suicide. In my soul I heard a sobering voice that stirred a decision to change my life once and for all. I cried, "Kill Me Not, you women sellers of illicit brews and drug addicts. I will never be a slave of your poisonous stuff!" Before I would have allowed myself to perish, God's plan prevailed and I surrendered my life to the LORD! I was freed from death, sin, and addiction. I could not control tears of joy from welling up in my eyes as I thanked God for freeing me.

Today I fight against drug abuse in my community. My campaign against this threatening menace is dubbed, "I Shall Not Die", "No More Death From Drug Abuse In Jesus's Name!"

To become this type of fighter, I needed to accept Jesus Christ as my personal savior in life. I was born again and completely transformed. I received a new life that affected me emotionally, mentally, spiritually, and physically. My friends were against my new lifestyle, arguing that it would not last. Some of them looked at me as if I was a stricken buffalo that had left the herd. I was a totally different person standing before them.

I was enjoying my new life in Christ by singing hymns instead of pop music. I enjoyed church services, events, and fellowships. Through Jesus Christ, I found answers to all of my problems. I shall never forget this phenomenon that occurred for myself.

Without the fear that someone may kill me, I described to my opposed friends that I was a victim from a battlefield who had found an escape route from a prolonged bombardment. I felt much unspeakable joy and peace of mind as I realized that God loves me.

After the death of my father from the consumption of the illicit brews, I focused on alcoholics and drug addicts. I started going around the village preaching the gospel and speaking out about the illicit brews.

I targeted young people in schools and in colleges because they are particularly vulnerable. Recently, six people, including teenagers, had died after consuming a lethal brew in Nakuru and Nyandarua. Two of them underwent treatment at the hospital while four others died before even arriving at the medical facilities.

There were another two people who were undergoing treatment at a health facility, a thirty-year-old man and a twenty-four-year-old woman, who lost their sight. Speaking at his bed, the young man told about how he had consumed several cups of the lethal brew in flight over an area of Nyandarua County. He explained, "I first started feeling weak, so I overslept then woke up only to realize that I could not see well." He had consumed the illicit brew known as "kabarito." He later thanked God after regaining his sight. After many such incidents, a father of a four-month-old boy promised me that he would quickly stop drinking the toxic drinks.

After preaching the gospel to the victims and praying for them, some of them came to be in a stable-enough condition that they could afford to compare notes; recalling events that almost brought their lives to an end. Most of them promised me that they would keep away from illicit brews from then on, saying they were satisfied that they had learn their lesson, despite it having to happen in a very hard and risky way.

In Trans-Nzoia County, one man talked about his regret after he went blind after consuming the toxic liquor called "shakers" worth fifty Ksh at a pub in Sibanga Market. After he had taken the brew as a refreshment, it took away his sight. The victim vowed, "I thank God

that I am alive. This marks the end of my drinking habit."

In Makueni County, the government pledged to cater for the medical and funeral expenses of poisonous drink victims. Sixteen people died after consuming illicit brews in the Kithuke ward. Public health workers had to close down the bars that were selling the illegal alcohol, proclaiming that they would be inspecting all drinks in the market to prevent a repeat of this tragedy.

The country has been experiencing many weekly deaths over the consumption of illicit brews. They have killed many people in different counties. More than a thousand survivors are still admitted in hospitals for consuming toxic drinks. The government has been on high alert over the tragedies caused by killer drinks whose samples have laced Ethanol. Some of the manufacturers, distributors, and sellers of second-generation brews have been forced to close down their businesses by the government. That's why I joined the government in their fight against illicit brews and drug abuse, and I am asking all Kenyans to join in this fight.

I am aggressively rescuing the youth. Let me ask you this question: Why would you want to risk dying before bringing up your children? Why would you allow greedy people to kill you with their toxic drinks and drugs? I want you to declare with me, "No more deaths from drug abuse in Jesus's name. KILL ME NOT!

I am leading the greatest campaign in the country against killer drinks and drugs; it is dubbed "I SHALL NOT DIE." I will not allow anybody to kill me with their toxic drinks or drugs. I am protected by the blood of Jesus Christ. The Bible explains to us who our real enemy is. In John 10:10, Jesus called the devil a thief. "The thief comes to steal, kill, and destroy." In order for him to accomplish his mission of stealing, killing, and destroying our lives, he uses tricks, lies, traps, and snares.

Jesus was brought upon us so that He may save you from the powers of the devil. He came so that we may have a life and have it to the fullest. Declare to the devil and everybody else, "Kill Me Not!"

Question: Are you a sinner, terminally ill, a drunkard, a drug addict, a coronavirus victim, an AIDS victim, a sex pervert, or a slave of the devil in any way?

It is unfortunate that it often takes hopeless situations for human beings to become open to listening to God's voice. Because of this, it might be possible that God could be directing your life towards an extreme situation or event in order to be able to make Himself known to you, as it may be the only way for Him to. However, God's will be on people's behalf. The devil brings about such extremes for the purpose of making people suffer and die.

From my experience, I can assure you that out of your present distress, our God can bring you to your greatest deliverance from your problems, diseases, situations, sins, or bondage. When I surrendered my miserable life to God as a drug addict, I was totally freed from death, sin, and addiction. I was completely changed. Today I am a preacher of the gospel. My mission is rescuing the youth from drug abuse, death, sins, diseases, and bondage.

If you truly believe, God's redeeming love is ready to touch you now and free you from the powers of the devil. Jesus invites you to come. As a regular visitor of our colleges and universities in Kenya, I have noticed that drug and substance abuse has been on the increase. These evil vices have resulted in many high-risk behaviors, such as poor academic performance and engaging in crimes, unprotected sexual intercourse, violence, and destruction of properties.

Substance abuse refers to the harmful or hazardous use of psychoactive substances, including alcohol, illicit drugs, and illicit brews. The use of psychoactive substances can lead to dependence syndrome — a cluster of behavioral, cognitive, and physiological phenomena that develop after repeated substance use. Victims suffer from a strong desire to take drugs, difficulties in controlling their use, persisting in their use despite harmful consequences, and an incentive to give higher priority to drug use above other activities and obligations.

On Fridays, students in universities organize parties, and a party is not a party without drugs. Many of them smoke bhang, the locally grown drug, and others use hard drugs such as heroin and cocaine. Unfortunately, most of these parties end up in fights and other ugly incidents, such as rape. The police say that every Saturday morning, they receive many cases of rape and violence as a result of drug-fueled parties from universities.

As a former addict and now as a minister of the gospel in the country, I can say that the current trend of drug and substance abuse among the youths in universities is a major national concern, as it has been reported to pose injurious effects on their health and academic performance. Many students die every day due to drug and alcohol-related complications. According to reports, the most widely abused drugs among students are alcohol, tobacco, bhang, marijuana, opium, cocaine, and heroin.

In Kenya, half of the drug abusers are aged between sixteen and twenty-eight years. Another severe problem in our institutions of higher learning is the menace that is illicit brew. Students have turned their dormitories into drinking dens. This trend has a sharp increase on indiscipline cases with deadly attacks, fights, and deaths of students.

There are two common types of illicit brews: "chang'aa" and "simba waragi." The latter is smuggled into the country from Uganda through the Busia border.

Simba waragi has taken students at Maseno University by storm. It is packed in polythene sachets and sold to students from twenty-five to thirty K sh. It is so popular that it has killed the once-dominant illicit brew chang'aa operation in that area.

No student wakes up one day and decides that they are going to abuse drugs. They must be introduced to this evil habit by a friend. I was introduced into alcohol consumption by my parents and into drug abuse by a friend. It started as fun, and later I became addicted. That is why I am always willing to rescue the drug addicts from these harmful behaviors. I like helping victims, especially the youth, to come out from this deadly vice.

For the addicts, I have counseling seminars in schools, colleges, and universities. My campaign against drug abuse is "I Shall Not Die." I advise the youth to use their time wisely, for time lost will never be recovered. I am calling for an urgent intervention by concerned experts to address this ticking time bomb of university students getting lured into drug addiction at an early stage.

Let's join hands to rescue this crooked generation from evil behaviors before it is too late. I always wondered why and how "good-looking" male students could use their bodies to do evil things like rape and other crimes instead of concentrating on their studies to become the charismatic future leaders that the world is waiting for? Why should female students be lured into fornication or engage themselves in prostitution instead of concentrating in their studies?

Question: Why would you want to die prematurely? I can remember one day after a drug spree when I missed death by a whisker. But before I got lost entirely to addiction, God's love arrested me the moment I decided to receive Jesus Christ as my personal savior. I was totally changed and transformed.

My life before I was born again was miserable and hopeless. It seemed as if I was brought up in a family of terrorists who wanted to kill me by giving me chang'aa to drink at an early age.

My life was very complicated because my parents were drunkards. If you play with fire, you will surely get burnt. I therefore decided to call upon Jesus Christ to save me from the jaws of the devil. The devil was pushing me to the grave, and one day I was lying in a near-death condition. An uprising was looming in the village; the devil was chasing me through my drug addiction, wanting to annihilate me. "Kill me not!" I cried.

Chapter 5

MY CAMPAIGN

MY TURNING POINT CAME when I got tired of living that miserable life. My cash drained out, and I began reflecting on how I had fallen into the bottomless pit of despair. This ignited a desire in me to reform. When I called Jesus Christ, he came into my soul, and I was transformed.

I told my family and friends that I shall not die; I will live for Jesus and preach the gospel to this hurting world. Today I am a full-time pastor who is giving motivational talks, counseling, and seminars to the youth against drug abuse.

I don't want to see the youth falling into the trap of drug addiction like I had. I believe that all victims of addiction will be set free in Jesus's name and others will never get trapped. As I live, I will fight and be ready to rescue the youth from drug abuse before it is too late. I am sure that one day in our family and in our communities, people will no longer die of alcohol-related causes or from HIV/AIDS. Tell your friends and everybody else who is concerned, "Kill me not," and, "I will not die." I am living for Christ to preach the gospel in this hurting world.

Because my parents were drunkards, I did not experience comfort, parental love, or guidance at home. I was brought up in a very humble way in life. My mother tried hard to educate my siblings and me through the very hard and risky means of brewing illicit brews at night. My brother and I used to ride a bicycle to Kiondo, Murogi, and Mithonge to sell the brand to retailers. This outlawed business was the lifeline of our family's income. As children, we were willing participants in this illegal business in the name of survival.

We siblings all started drinking at a tender age. When we grew up and became teenagers, we drifted into the meaningless life of abusing drugs. I had obtained many physical injuries to my body. I was hopeless and useless. "If only my anguish could be weighed, and all my misery placed on the scale! It could surely outweigh the sand of the seas" (Job 6:2–3).

I was a complete wreck and social misfit. Because of addiction, my body was aching and my mind was enslaved. I could not make a proper decision. I was mentally disturbed, even though I had thought I was smarter than my friends. In and out of school, I was hopeless. I was always thinking of committing suicide. But before I could perish forever in hell, God's redeeming love stopped me. I decided to receive Jesus Christ as my personal savior.

I was transformed. I was entirely changed from a drug addict into a gospel messenger. I crossed over from death to eternal life. I moved from my status as part of a crooked generation into my new state as part of a chosen generation. That is why my vision is to reach the lost and give hope to the hopeless. Today I preach the gospel to the sick, the poor, the rich, students, business people, officials, and prisoners.

I have written this book in good faith to help drug addicts, alcoholics, and other sinners to know that they can find deliverance and new lives, sober lives, as Christians. You can find answers in your troubled life after reading this book.

My testimony of how I was freed from addictions has encouraged victims to receive Jesus Christ as their personal savior. This book is written to give hope to many victims so that they will believe in the gospel. Through seminars and my campaign against drug abuse, I am targeting villages, estates, slums, and ghettos where you can find victims of illicit brews and their illicit brewers.

We help victims with concise and informative films that address their problems. I am teaching victims how to face reality and how to overcome stress, depression, frustration, hopelessness, and poverty, all damaging consequences of drug addiction. That's why our church, "Gospel Messengers Church," offers counseling sessions and deliverance meetings for the victims who are wanting to become totally transformed.

We organize rehabilitation programs for those who are not fully delivered, and after some time, transformation is realized. Our broad objective is to identify, recruit, counsel, and rehabilitate the victims of drug abuse. We also try to reach victims of rape, domestic violence, and sex workers through our outreach programs. We are also reaching students and pupils in schools, colleges, and universities.

In Kenya, the most destructive drug in general use is alcohol. Alcoholism has become the most pressing national problem in our country. We have millions who are confirmed alcohol victims. Children and youths are increasingly using alcohol and drugs. Most of our pupils in schools and students in colleges and universities are drinking. Pupils and students try drinking or use drugs for fun. Some drink to show off. Others drink to relieve tension or forget their worries, while others drink to escape reality. Unfortunately, once the pupil or student becomes hooked on drugs or alcohol, he or she becomes an addict. Addiction is a relapsing condition; most people with this problem have an underlying cause.

When one is affected by this condition, it is difficult for him or her to achieve life expectancy, goals, and intentions. Therefore, he or she cannot establish sustainable development, including academic development. Drug abuse and alcoholism have become such a common problem in our learning institutions, both formal and informal, that our youths are failing to achieve their potential.

Many of our youths today have developed health problems that affect their minds and bodies. It has been clearly established that drugs and alcohol have led to the spread of HIV/AIDS in our learning institutions, causing many premature deaths. Our youth engage themselves in casual relationships that cause the death of one or both partners after betrayal. Many students have killed their partners, committing suicide later. Students are caught in crime because of abusing drugs and alcohol.

Drug and alcohol abuse makes you lose your self-control, as in your inhibition, as well as the ability to make sound decisions; such that you do not feel too cautious to engage in risky behaviors. Intoxication diminishes your perception of what is risky. In this unfortunate state of mind, you can allow yourself to participate in dangerous sexual conduct with a high risk of HIV infection.

Intoxication gives the abuser a false sense of enhanced sexual arousal and performance. This excitement or high mood accompanied by false courage often leads to risky sexual behavior. You become likely to engage in high-risk sexual activity that involves sleeping around with multiple sex partners, engaging in unprotected sexual activities, or exchanging in sex for money or drugs.

Alcohol is killing people faster than the deadliest wars of history. It is killing victims in cities, towns, and villages. Most of us have heard sad stories from our schools, colleges, and universities about how these young people are dabbling with drugs and alcohol. It is unfortunate to hear that most of our youngsters are drug abusers, criminals, or murderers.

It is true that most of our young people try their first glass of alcohol or their first sniff or puff out of curiosity. But later, the experience turns out to be hooking and devastating. That's why you find victims in counties, cities, towns, and villages looking frantically for more drugs or alcohol. Once the victim becomes hooked, you could find him or her breaking into apartments or stealing from homes or stores in order to get money to buy more drugs.

Drugs affect both the mind and the body. Drugs can be taken into the body in different forms. They can be taken through the mouth, through the veins by a needle, inhaled into the lungs, or through the nose. Drugs affect the cells that form the organs of the body, such as the heart, brain, kidneys, etc.

Some drugs bring about emotional change. They affect your mind and feelings. Drugs also affect the central nervous system. Certain drugs can make one feel very excited or very alert. These are usually called "stimulants." Common stimulants that are abused include amphetamines, popularly known as "speed," or "uppers."

Other drugs can make one feel quieter and calmer. These are called "sedatives." Tobacco and alcohol are in this category. Addicts of alcohol find it difficult to relax in the evening without a glass of wine, a shot of whiskey, or an illicit brew. You'd start with one glass to make you feel relaxed. Still, after some time, you feel like relaxing with a bottle of wine to maintain the relaxation effect.

Another harmful drug is marijuana, which comes from the plant known as cannabis sativa. When people smoke marijuana, they exhibit an impairment of memory, have no concentration, and show poor work performance. It causes redness of the eyes, dryness of the mouth, distortion of senses, and an altered sense of consciousness.

Another harmful drug is LSD (Lysergic acid diethylamide), which causes hallucinations. The senses of sight, hearing, and touch are distorted. Victims may jump out of the window or over a steep cliff to commit suicide. Victims start suspecting harm from others. The drug contains mescaline, which produces hallucinations. Many victims abuse these drugs called "hallucinogens."

Amphetamines (stimulants) are drugs that tend to give the user energy, wake the user up, and make the user feel like he or she can do anything. Abusers take amphetamines to stay awake, keep alert, elevate their mood, increase their initiative, and give them confidence. One of the most abused stimulant drugs is cocaine.

Barbiturates (sedatives) are drugs that depress the action of the nerves and thus lead to sluggishness, difficulty in thinking, slowness of speech, poor memory, and faulty judgment. Symptoms of abuse include staggering and stumbling, falling asleep, a lack of interest in school, etc. All of these harmful drugs are sold by drug peddlers.

Opium and heroin (narcotics) are drugs that induce a state of narcosis or sleep. Opium is one of the oldest and most widely used of the narcotics. It is obtained from the milky substance in the poppy plant that is dried in several stages. The most potent opiate is heroin. This drug is generally taken into the system by injecting it into the body. The addict comes to the belief that he or she must continue to take the drug in order to feel normal. Heroin is a challenging drug from which to withdraw.

The most common drugs used illegally are psychedelic drugs like marijuana, narcotic drugs like heroin, and hallucinogenic drugs like LSD. When a drug abuser keeps on using drugs, his or her body comes to require an increasing amount of the drug to experience the desired effects. The body just keeps on demanding large amounts of doses, and in the case of the victim attempting to discontinue his or her use, he or she will suffer withdrawal effects when the next dose of the drug is not received within the given time.

The body keeps revolting, and several symptoms occur, including severe cramping, vomiting, chills, and profuse sweating. That's why I am warning abusers about just how harmful all of these drugs are to their health. These drugs have caused premature deaths to the addicts. Alcoholism and drug addiction are diseases that are hard to treat.

Are you an alcoholic or a drug addict? As a former addict and a pastor now, I am willing to help you in my pastoral counseling program. Join our counseling seminars, and we shall connect you with Jesus, who will help you through your addictions. In our program, we shall help you with your drug or alcohol dependence to start a new life without the feeling of need for a drink, puff, or sniff.

Every addict is given a life-changing message from the Bible, which is from God's point of view. Those who use alcohol or drugs are not sick as much as sinful. And Jesus was crucified on the cross for our sins. If it is Jesus Christ who will set you free, you shall be free from every sin, bondage, and sickness. Drunkards are listed with thieves, liars, extortionists, and murderers. (1 Corinthians 6:9–10).

The Bible says that alcohol bites. "At the last, it bites like a serpent and stings like an adder" (Proverbs 23:32). Don't be deceived by drinking alcohol. "Wine is a mocker; a strong drink is raging, and whoever is deceived thereby is not wise" (Proverbs 20:1).

Drunkards will not inherit the kingdom of God. The best treatment for alcoholics and drug addicts is accepting deliverance (Luke 4:18). Through our pastoral counseling program, we would lead you into a deliverance class where we'd minister to you and pray for you. You would then become totally freed from all kinds of addictions.

Jesus invites you to salvation and deliverance when he asks you to. "Come unto me, all ye that labor and are heavily laden, and I will give you rest" (Matthew 11:28). Why not believe God's word now and become set free from your heavy addictions? Call Jesus Christ now to save you.

Drugs and illicit brews give their victims a false sense of well-being. Afterward, the abusers suffer a lot of pain when trying to withdraw without the help of the super powerful Jesus Christ. When Jesus Christ sets you free, you are guaranteed to be freed forever.

I have seen Jesus Christ transform and free drug addicts completely. Victims are healed from committing suicide attempts, stress, and depression. They are set free from physical, emotional, mental, and spiritual problems. As a pastor and a former drug addict, I interview some drug addicts after their deliverance. Some tell me that they were suffering from depression, stress, anxiety, fear, loss of weight, lack of energy, or low libido. Others say they felt self-confidence and boldness in approaching situations after abusing drugs. As for me, I call all stuff of addiction, "madness."

In my seminars to the victims, I make sure that I give them the full dose of the word of God before I minister deliverance and healing. Without Jesus Christ as your personal savior, you cannot be freed or transformed. There is no shortcut.

I have led thousands of victims to deliverance, and they are becoming sober Christians and business people. Rescuing the victims from drugs can transform them into good Christian citizens. We are helping the transformed youth to start income-generating projects, which helps them fight poverty, hopelessness, and joblessness in their lives. We are giving them life-changing skills in this outreach project. Join us in this project and declare together what the word of God says:

"I shall not die, but I will live to declare the works of the Lord."

My vision is to reach the lost and give hope to the hopeless. Thank God that I was rescued from death, sins, and addictions. My ministry is helping drunkards, drug addicts, and other sinners to be delivered from death, sins, and addictions. Please don't join the losers in hell. Just trust Jesus as your savior, and you will live in heaven forever.

By the grace of God, I am saved, and by believing in Jesus Christ, I survived death by a whisker. I have written this book to warn sinners, drunkards, and addicts not to allow themselves to be in such a state that would condemn them to hell. Jesus is the answer. My living testimony has helped my sisters and mother to accept Jesus Christ as their personal savior.

Unfortunately, my father refused to accept Him. Father was always finding excuses, and he had his moment where he was looking for a place to hide from the accusations and guilt of his own conscience. There is no type of moment I know of that disturbs human beings more nowadays or is harder to bear: the torment of an accusing conscience is so full of anguish. To soothe his conscience from accusation, my father used to crack jokes with his mates in the drinking dens all day.

He would tell them that he would stop drinking the illicit brew when he dies. But, he ultimately indeed continued to drink until he died. Alcoholism had destroyed his health and made him bedridden in the hospital for months. The doctor warned him to stop drinking, but when he returned home from the hospital, he still drank. A few days later, he died at home from what the doctor called cirrhosis, a liver disease.

Alcohol causes a decrease in brain activity, and in time, it can result in heart disease, cirrhosis, and other fatal diseases. Tobacco contains nicotine. Nicotine tends to calm the nerves. It is often the cause of lip, mouth, and throat cancer. Smokers shorten their lives after smoking.

My father died a drunkard and a hopeless parent. He died a sinner like the rich man in Luke 16:19–31. The Bible tells us about the rich man and a poor man named Lazarus. The rich man lived in pleasure and in sin, but the poor man, Lazarus, feared God and lived in righteousness. They both died naturally, but the rich man was condemned to hell to eternally burn in the lake of fire while the poor man, Lazarus, was carried by angels to Abraham's bosom, where he would enjoy eternal life.

Question: After your death, where will you spend eternity? Are you a drug addict or alcoholic? We have heard stories of some victims becoming blind or impotent and many others dying because of their addictions. These risky substances destroy the nervous system, which can cause their victims to die. God has given everybody the free will to choose life or death; blessings or curses. I have chosen life. In my office, you will find my motto written in red that says, "I SHALL NOT DIE."

Believers are encouraged and built up to find these letters in my office. These attention-gripping words, which I send through social media, are reminders to the whole world. I have been receiving reports of encouragement from victims from all around the world who are testifying about how they have felt transformed after reading my story of deliverance.

My story is a timely reminder to the world that God can change a drug addict and use him or her to reach victims for Christ. That's why I focused on my vision. The Bible encourages me, "You shall declare a thing and shall be established" (Job 22:28).

This is why I declare that the drug addicts and alcoholics shall be set free from addiction and sins in Jesus's name. God will wipe the tears of sisters, brothers, and relatives of victims who had lost their lives because of addiction. I declare that "cursed" are the illicit brew sellers and drug peddlers. I declare that there shall be no more domestic violence in their homes and families.

The Bible says, "Give a strong drink to he who is perishing and wine to those in better distress. Let them drink and forget their poverty and remember their misery no more" (Proverbs 31:6). God had set me free from death, sins, and addictions. Jesus said, "I tell you the truth. Whoever hears my word and believes Him who has sent me has eternal life and will not be condemned. He'll be crossed over from death to life" (John 5:24). When I declared my belief that Jesus was to be my personal savior, I crossed over from death to life.

The word encourages me, "I am the resurrection and the life. He who believes in me will live forever even though he dies, and whoever lives and believes in me will never die. Do you believe this?" (John 11:25–26). That's why I believe that I shall not die but instead have eternal life with Jesus.

I am targeting students in schools, colleges, universities, and youth in general. I advise students to maintain a good relationship with their teachers and their parents. They should also learn how to handle disagreements on issues with their teachers to avoid unnecessary strikes and acts of destruction to properties. Strikes affect their performance in class as well as their well-being.

I teach students behaviors to understand who they are in Christ and to be examples in all things. I teach them how to respect their teachers and work to achieve their objectives in case of any problem, as students should communicate with teachers effectively. Every student should trust their teachers and learn to obey their orders. They should be humble, positive thinkers who have time to relax and, most importantly, learn to listen.

Trusting Jesus helps students to overcome stress, which is very common with students. The word of God has the power to energize and motivate you, as well as help you overcome trials, temptations, or challenges in school and at home.

Stress can cause severe psychological and physical problems. A high level of stress can lead you to depression. Are you tempted to try drugs or alcohol as a means to overcome your stress? Be realistic in dealing with your present problems. Are you anxious, irritable, or stressed? Are you losing interest in life? Are you a student becoming uninterested in performing your studies? Are you feeling tired all the time? Do you feel like withdrawing socially? Do you have trouble concentrating? You could be suffering from stress.

Call Jesus Christ into your heart right now and confess your sins. You can be healed and freed from sin and stress.

In Kenya, the church is helping the government to carry out its mandate to create a secure environment for social-economic development, but alcohol and drug abuse has emerged as a major social challenge and a threat to national security. Crime is very high in rural areas, as well as in urban areas. Substance abuse is emerging as a severe security challenge for the general population.

The youth are the most affected, and this poses a serious threat to the productivity of the working-age group in our country. Because of the rapid increase in alcohol consumption and drug abuse, the youth have been engaging in crime as a way of raising funds to sustain their drug-dependent lifestyle at the expense of engaging in productive endeavors. In addition to being hazardous to health, drugs are causing our youth to engage in crimes such as rape, assault, suicide, and many other types of criminal activities.

However, despite this, the government is fighting hard to end this menace. The government is eradicating the most destructive alcohol, known as the "generational brews." These brews are mostly packaged in plastic bottles and sold in bars as wines and spirits. These dangerous brews are causing deaths and other health complications to the consumers.

The consumption of the second-generation brews has worsened the situation. As a consequence, the country has witnessed widespread road accidents caused by drivers abusing drugs and the second-generation brews, which are easily mixed with a soda or mineral water. While traveling using public means, you may see the matatu (the bus drivers) drinking this dangerous stuff in the form of soda or water in a bottle. You wouldn't suspect the driver is drinking while driving.

I'm protesting that such drivers, who are risking the lives of travelers, should be taken to court and have their driving licenses revoked. This move would reduce road carnage in our country. I am concerned seeing reckless drivers killing people every day on our roads. Lane division used to help drivers, but drunken drivers do not stay in their lanes.

The Murogi village is the most notorious spot, with all forms of crimes and all types of antisocial behavior. There has been an increase in drug addiction, prostitution, and other forms of evil activities. I have noticed that illicit brews and prostitution go together in the ghettos.

As a pastor, I have said that I am not going to just sit and watch people perishing because of drug abuse. I am going to rescue them before it is too late. I am willing to work with NACADA in its campaign against drug abuse. I am eager to educate the youth and the public on the dangers of drug abuse, alcoholism, and sexual immorality. I am willing to start rehabilitation programs in the estates. I wish to reiterate that the fight against drug abuse and the consumption of illicit brews should be handled through teamwork and partnership of the counties.

My main objective is to bring positive behavior changes in the sexual relations of the youth in order to reduce the risk of HIV/AIDS transmissions. My resource materials include films and video shows with Christian and moral values portrayed in them. Accompanying me is a team of counselors who help me in teaching, evaluating, monitoring, and responding to the questions asked by participants.

This project is very effective in reducing drug abuse and educating about what causes the most significant risk of HIV/AIDS transmission in the youth. I am calling to the NGOs and the government to help me in making these visions a reality. My question is: Why would you want to die prematurely? My campaign is dubbed, "I shall not die."

We help the men who are alcoholics to stop their drinking. Many marriages end in divorce because of husbands coming home past midnight lying to their wives that they were watching football when they were actually drinking with friends.

Chapter 6

WHERE WILL YOU SPEND ETERNITY?

VERONICAH WAS THE NAME given to my mother when she embraced religion as a Roman Catholic Christian; a committed follower of Christianity. One year after my brother, Dominic, died, the gospel was preached to her by members of our church, "Gospel Messengers Church." She accepted Jesus Christ as her personal savior and joined our church.

As a committed believer, my mother went through effort to understand the will of God in her life. She used to attend all meetings, Sunday services, and mid-week fellowships of believers. She loved the "keshas," the overnight vigil meetings held once a month.

My mother was always led by the spirit and Word of God, which she devotedly obeyed in her Christian life. She proclaimed that she would keep her faith and conscience and focused on doing the will of

God. She was always the first to give for missions and projects.

In September 2015, the heart condition she had worsened. She was taken to St. Mary's hospital in Gilgil. After a few months, the shadow of death was hovering over her, and one day she stopped breathing. But, she died peacefully. Many people, including family members, relatives, friends, believers, and pastors, attended her burial ceremony.

The Bible encourages us, "Precious in the sight of the Lord is the death of His saints" (Psalm 116:15). My mum was a precious saint in our church. Although she left us suddenly, her prayers were still working for her children, grandchildren, and the church.

From the day she accepted Jesus Christ, she lived a better life, with members of the church and her neighbors. In the village, she was a very successful farmer who kept livestock for her livelihood. She lived in the Kiambogo village until the day she met her death.

The Kiambogo village is about forty-five kilometers from the Town of Nakuru and thirty-five kilometers from the Town of Gilgil. It is surrounded by the Eburu Forest from the east, which is the home of famous and many kinds of wild animals. Often, in the village at night, you could hear herds of buffalo from the Eburu Forest invading our crops. That's why the village was given the name, "Kiambogo," which means, "a village of many buffalos."

In the village, you could quickly note an acute water shortage during the dry seasons. Dams and rivers would be dry due to the prolonged drought. Women and girls would be forced to walk long distances in search of a commodity.

Many times, my mother used to retreat in prayer in what she called a "prayer season." She felt the Holy Spirit urging her to pray for her family and her church. She would wake up very early, leaving her bed unmade, dishes unwashed, livestock unfed, and garden unattended as she waited upon the Lord in prayer. She was an intercessor. When I visited her, she would tell me that she was "in prayer mood." I could hear her saying prayers and in them mentioning all her children, grandchildren, and church members by their names.

Writing my mum's story was not easy because members of the family are still agonizing over the loss of her. She had brought us, her children, up for more than sixty-six years, helping us to survive in this hurting world. Mama, as we called her in our family, was a pillar to us. She was very understanding, caring, loving, and compassionate— everything we could ask for in a mother.

When she would kneel down to pray, her prayers would work miracles in our lives. You could hear her praying and mentioning all the ministers of the gospel. She also prayed for other churches. She prayed for me and my ministry.

I was my mum's pastor and mentor. She told God to sanctify me wholly and preserve me as blameless until the second coming of Jesus Christ. Sometimes when preaching on a Sunday service, she would shout, "That's true! Say it all!"

She advised me to preach messages that would build and add value to the souls of the congregation. She stood very firm in her spiritual convictions. She encouraged believers with her moving testimonies, which she would tell of without fear. She encouraged me to start a church ministry in her village. Whenever the church stood up to praise and worship, she would go forward in the pulpit to join the praise and worship team. She believed that she was called to praise the Lord.

The whole congregation admired her unique dancing style. She meant business in the service to God. She encouraged her in-laws and her grandchildren and always stood with them in prayer during challenging times.

She endured and brought my siblings and me up even when our dad died in 1984. My sister died in the year 2000 and my brother in 2003. Despite all this, she remained strong in her faith until her last minute.

Many believers, relatives, family members, friends, and neighbors came to celebrate the life of a precious saint. A life well lived. During her burial, speeches, eulogy, and tributes were read by family members, grandchildren, and believers. Her burial was led by Bishop Tinkoi from Ngong, Nairobi. He read from the book of John 14:3: "And when I go and prepare a place for you, I will come again and will take you to myself, that where I am you may also be."

The bishop gave many life illustrations to describe the beautiful life beyond the grave. He knew my mum. To us, the family members, this was a very important day in our lives. The text had special significance to us and had a great revelation to us.

Before the burial, we had spent the whole night with spiritual leaders discussing the right person to lead the burial service. All of the spiritual leaders remembered how Mum used to give them gifts, prepare food for them, and make beds for them as guests. Her house was small, but she always made sure that her guests were comfortable.

We felt blessed when the bishop spoke about my mother because he had visited her a few days before her death. He told the mourners that my mother had said to him that she knew her house in heaven was ready and that she was waiting for the day to come when she would enter it.

When the bishop ended the sermon, he called us as a family to the front for prayers and encouragement. It was not easy for us, but God helped us to endure it. We remained silent as the anointing from the bishop flowed through our souls as he prayed for us.

After the prayers, the bishop led us to the grave, where we laid the body of my mother, the precious saint. The bishop helped us to bury her with great peace and celebration. We gave our mother a wonderful send-off. We thanked our friends and our family members as they left the burial site with cheerful faces.

Our family was comforted by the word of God: "Yea, though I walk through the valley of the shadow of death, I will fear no evil, for you are with me; your rod and your staff, they comfort me" (Psalm 23:4).

I am comforted to know that Jesus does not make mistakes. He knows all my needs, troubles, and sorrow. He knows my name, and he calls upon me by it. Jesus knew me when I was still in my mother's womb. He knows me from my childhood up to now. He never mistakes me for someone else. Jesus knows me well.

<u>To Her Children</u>

My mother always blessed and wished all her children well. She had taught us endless and priceless values. Despite her real daily example of living, she taught us how to love, share, care, and forgive, and more importantly, how to treat every person well. She was our family's role model. She encouraged her children to emulate Jesus Christ and keep their faith to the end.

<u>To Her Grand Children</u>

I'm sure everyone who called her "Cucu," meaning "grandmother," has memories concerning her—good memories. Something they will always love to cherish. It was very often that when they would visit her, they would experience the love of the old woman who was very special to them. She would guide them as they called her "Cucu." And no matter how many times they felt messed up, her heart was always opened for them.

She taught the boys how to behave like good men and the girls how to act like good women. All of the children were taught to endure life and live without complaining. They were taught how to overcome youthful lusts by believing in Jesus Christ.

This kind of "cucu" who loves so many people so unconditionally and without discrimination is very hard to find. She may not have approved of everything they did, but she appreciated them without judgment.

Whenever they needed her, she was always there for them. She would listen, comfort, and encourage them. She lived a simple life with her livestock. It did not take much to make her happy. A glass of milk, a piece of roasted meat, a phone call, a small gift, a visit, or a task well done is all you needed to put a smile on her face. And she wanted all her grandchildren to do their best in their studies.

Money can be squandered and property ruined, but what they inherited from their "cucu" cannot be damaged, destroyed, or lost. It is permanent, and it keeps her from becoming just a pleasant memory; it keeps her alive in their hearts forever.

<u>To Her Great Grand Children.</u>

To all who called her "maitu," you indeed lost quite a special person in your life. "Maitu" means "great-grandmother." I know I always felt loved, wanted, and special by her. She made your childhood very special. Some of the best memories you have are of being with her. It did not matter what she was doing; she always spent quality time with you.

Your "maitu" played with you, chatted with you all night, and joked with you. She was always loving, compassionate, determined, and caring. I'm sure that you were touched by her love. You always felt proud to be with her.

Remember the songs and chorus she sang for you as you waited for supper or lunch. How she prayed for you; asking God to grant you wisdom in your schooling so that you may be able to differentiate fact from fiction and perceive the truth. She told you that one day she would go to heaven and that you would be granted that gift as well if you live your lives loving God and obeying His voice.

<u>To Neighbors</u>

My mother was relatively plump, a kind of woman who was considerably generous to the neighbors and relatives. She had a special gift of hospitality. She was very kind to all. Even though our resources were uncertain, Mother could always spare a cup of tea or a plate of food for any unexpected visitor.

Mother was eloquent in her speeches, and she was always praying for her neighbors and friends. She believed that everything can be made possible through prayer. With prayers, no burden could not be lifted, no storm could not be calmed, no sorrow could not be erased, and nobody could not be saved.

She prayed for broken marriages to be restored. She called all the villagers to come and drink the waters of life, but they ignored it. She believed that the gospel had to be preached in the villages so that sinners could be saved. There had never been a day in her life when she did not mention sinners who still needed to be saved. With her prayers, she attacked the kingdom of darkness as she pulled down the strongholds.

My mother had indeed gone to rest from her labors, trials, and tribulations in this hurting world. She is now in heaven, where she wished to be in order to be free from death, pain, and sorrow.

Mum walked in her eighty-six years of a long journey of life with passion and determination to be like Christ. She went to be with the Lord on 9/21/2015.

Today, I choose to keep alive in my memories my mother's life, strength, passion, wisdom, and golden heart. Our mother was our pillar in life, and after her death, our heroine. She will be greatly missed by her children, friends, relatives, neighbors, and ministers of the gospel.

Gospel Messengers Church will never forget the powerful prayers of our mother. She is one of the founders of our ministry. Rest in peace! Fare thee well, Mum! We gave our mother a wonderful sendoff. My mother is in heaven. Where will you spend eternity?

Chapter 7

RESCUING THE YOUTH FROM DRUG ABUSE

WE REACH DRUG ADDICTS and alcoholics through seminars in schools, colleges, towns, villages, estates, slums, and ghettos. On November 25, 2020, we registered "Stay Up Rehabilitative

Community-Based Organization," this being a vital project in the Kiambogo location, Elementaita Ward, Gilgil District, and Nakuru County.

We are using Christian films, videos, books, charts, posters, and leaflets in our outreach seminars. We have twelve facilities, and Mr. Daniel Kuto is one of the facilitators. Apart from being a teacher in school, he has a diploma in counseling.

The main objectives of this outreach project are to:

• Teach the community about the dangers of drug abuse and alcoholism.

• Rehabilitate people to start income-generating projects that could keep them busy to avoid being hooked in addiction again.

- Encourage the victims to maintain salvation and healing in the church.

We are working in collaboration with the administration in our area, as well as spiritual leaders, doctors, and school teachers, to reach the communities. We are trying to locate a big plot where we will build a permanent building that will be a center for rehabilitation for addicts and alcoholics.

We are encouraging former addicts to start simple businesses to alleviate hopelessness, idleness, poverty, and crime in society. In our outreach projects, there are some factors that are hindering moral development in our area, which include poverty, unemployment, and illiteracy, as well as cultural and traditional beliefs.

Despite this, Gospel Messengers Church has been playing a very important role in providing spiritual counseling to all those victims. To bring word out to our vision and campaign, we are kindly requesting all stakeholders, NGOs, the government, and county governments to partner with us to end this destructive menace in society.

We need funds to buy teaching devices, e.g., laptops, tablets, projectors, and tents, for this outreach project. We also need a van for transporting our facilitators to the seminar venues and a pickup system to carry equipment like public address in the venues. Our staff will continue to do follow-ups, as well as monitoring and evaluation in villages, estates, and schools. We need funds to help those victims who have been rehabilitated to start income-generating businesses for their survival.

We are to spread awareness to reduce drug abuse. That is why we are promoting sobriety in our community. We are targeting the youth in the society. Please partner with us in our campaign against this destructive vice that is threatening our youth and the communities.

Help us to rescue many victims before it is too late.

What has the world come to? Everybody is asking this in this hurting world. Recently I sat beside the fireplace opposite of my family deeply considering the condition we are in. We are staying in the house for fear of COVID-19, the newly discovered coronavirus pandemic that seems to be life's greatest disaster.

The doctors are telling us that human coronaviruses were first characterized in the 1960s and are responsible for a substantial number of cases of upper respiratory tract infections in people. Since 2003, at least five new human coronaviruses have been identified, and they originated from bats. This is one of the most dangerous pandemics that is spreading very fast from person to person and is causing many deaths daily around the world.

Most people infected with the COVID-19 virus will experience fever or cough in mild to moderate respiratory illness. There are people who became infected while traveling abroad and others who became infected after having close contact with a victim known to be infected with the virus but without knowing how or where he or she had been infected.

The best way to prevent and slow down transmission is to be well informed about the COVID-19 virus and the danger it causes. Please try hard to prevent yourself and others from getting infected by washing your hands with soap and running water frequently and not touching your face. Wearing a cloth face covering is not a substitute to recommended social distancing. You should keep about six feet between yourself and others. If you have a fever or cough you should go to the nearest health center.

The COVID-19 virus spreads primarily through droplets of saliva or discharge from the nose when an infected person coughs or sneezes, so it is important that you also practice respiratory etiquette (for example, by coughing into a flexed elbow).

You should be very careful because at this time there are no specific vaccines or treatment for COVID-19. However, there are many ongoing clinical trials evaluating potential treatments. The World Health Organization will continue to provide updates and information as soon as clinical findings become available.

There is no controversy—Jesus is Lord. This is a very clear message that should be preached in all corners of this hurting world. Jesus brought transformation because the whole world was condemned to eternal suffering. He won our acquittal. We were destined to die, but He gave us eternal life. He is the only one who came from Heaven to save the world from sins and diseases. His name is Jesus, the son of the living God.

Our rehabilitation center is different from the others you may know of because we use the Bible to help victims re-examine themselves. Because I was a drug addict before I gave my life to Jesus Christ, who saved and delivered me from addictions, I know how to love and help the victims of drug abuse.

I was brought up in a poverty-stricken family of four boys and five girls. I will never forget how my mother used to give me a glass of chang'aa when I'd come home from school instead of giving me lunch. After drinking, I'd fall asleep for hours on an empty stomach while she'd be selling the illicit brew to her customers.

By the age of fifteen years, every member of my family displayed all the symptoms of addiction. All my siblings and I were required to help Mother sell chang'aa in the brew dens. I was always sent to keep watch and to signal if the policemen were ever approaching. In return, I'd be given two glasses of chang'aa for a job well done.

At that tender age, I was drinking, smoking cigarettes, and taking bhang. My elder brother succumbed to drug addiction and became a nuisance. His evil habit caused the family to experience many heartaches, but whenever I tried stopping him, he would fight with me in the drinking den.

As a former drug addict, I have decided to help many victims and parents struggling with drug addictions. I have volunteered to help them. My family wallowed in ignorance about drug addiction. My brother and I were saved and transformed in the late seventies after receiving Jesus Christ in our lives.

Drug addiction disheartened me, so I decided to help addicts be set free from addictions. I am now a counselor for drug addicts. I am targeting young boys from the age of ten to thirty-five years because many young boys experiment with drugs, ignoring the fact that it could lead them to addiction, which is very hard to treat. I urge parents to help their children to recover from addiction.

Our first concern in this program is recovery from drug addiction. We talk to victims in the villages, slums, and ghettos who need recovery and promise them a new way of life. The survival of a victim depends on the promises of healing in our program. It is not until the victims come to our rehabilitation center that recovery becomes possible. This program works for all those victims who are willing to allow themselves to be set free from abuse and addiction.

Damaging Consequences

In my recent study, I found that drug abuse and illicit brew consumption in our area are the leading causes of domestic violence in many homes. Sexual violence is very high among young girls and women, the perpetrators being drug addicts and drunkards.

The Bible says, "Woe unto them who are mighty to drink wine and of strength to mingle strong drink" (Isaiah 5:22).

That's why I am going around to drinking dens and drinking parties to rescue victims from addiction and the psychological effects of drugs and drinking. Illicit brews are mixed with a very dangerous chemical called "methanol." The substance affects the victim's perception, mood, and consciousness. Victims become blind, and some die prematurely. Abusers become impotent. Drugs and illicit brew consumption cause damaging consequences by giving the victims a false sense of well-being. Afterward, the abuser suffers much pain when he or she tries to withdraw.

Some abusers are husbands who are unable to perform their duties at home and stay in bed. Wives suffer from frequent disagreements and fight about paying bills and buying basic needs instead of spending the little money they have on drugs and alcohol for their husbands. The effects of domestic violence range from physical, to social, to psychological. Wives claim that their husbands leave home very early to go to work, but instead of working, these men are actually spending all their time drinking the illicit brew sold in the estate or village. Drinking causes the husbands to come home empty-handed. Poor judgment on the part of the victim and the inability to provide for the family are the leading causes of domestic violence in many homes in our area today.

I have found that crimes are often very high during the holidays because teens are idle, and therefore they can be easily tempted into drug abuse, illicit brew consumption, and petty crimes. Crime and violence pervade the lives of many young people during the holiday seasons. Idleness causes the youth to engage in evil behaviors and watch pornographic movies.

These increased destructive behaviors by our youth are touching everybody in society. We should address this issue of drug and illicit brew consumption in our area completely. School dropouts often perpetrate violent and criminal acts because they are bitter about their status. They failed to continue school to get a college or university education, so they feel trapped and hopeless.

Rehabilitation Process

As a former drug addict, I have willingly volunteered to help addicts to come out from addiction. I want to enroll in a diploma program for addiction counseling. To my understanding, addiction is a fatal disease. That's what motivates me to educate society on the dangers of drug abuse.

Drug abuse exposes the victims to HIV/AIDS. One of our outreach programs directs the addicts to areas of deliverance, healing, and recovery. Advanced medical treatment and proper counseling make it possible for an addict to be healed and restored. The church needs funds and moral support to help addicts with medical treatment. The medical process of rehabilitation on addicts is a very expensive exercise, and you know that many addicts are hopeless and jobless and cannot afford the high fee charged in rehabilitation centers.

For example, the Mathare Rehabilitation Center in Nairobi is the cheapest, and it still charges 400 Ksh per day. Other private rehabilitation institutions charge 1000 Ksh per day. An addict is expected to pay between 60,000 Ksh and 140,000 Ksh for the full program.

That is why I have decided to help addicts receive total deliverance and healing and recovery by using Bible verses. Today I am committed to helping addicts and educating young children in school before they can become addicted. I am giving addicts the best treatment for addiction: Jesus Christ. I travel to the villages and estates to find addicts willing to be delivered biblically. I invite them to our church, which is our rehabilitation center. Before admission, they fill out a form first. After that, the program of healing lessons from the Bible kicks off.

Addicts are taught Bible verses on deliverance, healing, and salvation. After a time, they are led to accept Jesus Christ as their personal savior. The victims are totally delivered and healed. For some time, the former addicts must do some physical exercises and learn spiritual lessons on how to keep their healing and salvation. After former addicts are healed, we give them life-changing skills and encourage them to start small income-generating businesses. Many of them are now living drug-free lives as sober Christians.

This program is sponsored by our church and is free of charge. We are called to preach the gospel and give hope to the hopeless by showing the true love of Jesus Christ to sinners and the needy. My ministry is committed to eradicating the problems of addiction in society. We are sharing all spiritual techniques free of charge to any willing person or victim. We are appealing to our government and any willing NGO or person who will assist us in making this vision of reaching the unreached a reality.

Former addicts are giving us moving testimonies of their healing regardless of the duration of their addictions. There is healing in the blood of Jesus Christ. Victims are saying that the success of our wonderful program of rehabilitation is undeniable. Thousands of addicts recover from all signs of withdrawal and symptoms of dependence, e.g., yawning, feeling hot or cold, weakness, nausea, and vomiting. Former addicts tell me that they became set free from the craving, and their bodies become repelled by the smell of drugs and/or alcohol.

Recovery Process

The victims enroll to start this deliverance process. With much love, they are made to accept that they are in danger and in need of help. They begin to receive the kindness and God's love given in the program, where they are accepted as they are.

The victims are taught step by step the dangers of drug abuse and addictions using the Bible. They are taught steps to deliverance and healing. They are convinced that they cannot recover without the power of God. They are trained to admit that they need to receive Jesus Christ as their personal savior in order to be totally delivered and set free.

After deliverance, the victims are advised to join Gospel Messengers Church or any other Christian ministry to continue with Bible study lessons and fellowship meetings with members to further become strong in their faith. Without the Bible study and regular prayers, they cannot survive. With their strong faith in Jesus Christ, the incredible power of God, and love from believers, the good news of deliverance is carried to other addicts who are still suffering.

The desire to be set free is the basis of recovery from drug abuse and addiction. In the testimonies of the former addicts, this message is passed on to other addicts. We help those who are willing to be delivered. Some addicts can be analyzed, counseled, prayed over, threatened, beaten, or locked up, yet can never stop abusing drugs.

Healing Process

We invite doctors to help those addicts who don't want our Bible-based healing or deliverance from addiction. The only thing we ask of the addicts before we take them into our rehabilitation center is that they must have the desire to be delivered. The *desire* to be set free is the first requirement of our program although we have opened doors for all addicts. This program is open to all men and women who have agreed to follow the spiritual principles needed to find true freedom from addiction and receive a new way of life.

We have two types of fellowship meetings. The first one is open for other church members, and the other one is closed for former addicts only. This makes my work of monitoring their progress easier, as I can clearly see how much support each one needs.

We help our new members, the former addicts, to make amends with those who were hurt or injured by their former behavior derived from drug abuse. We guide them on how they can overcome guilt and live in total inner peace. They must be ready to learn how to ask for forgiveness from their family members and others offended by their evil behaviors. Many admit that they had caused much harm to their families.

Through prayers and Bible study, the former addicts improve their conscious contact with God, and our regular meetings increase their spiritual growth and healing. We make sure that they meet many times to discuss their faith and spiritual development. God will never force His blessing to us. We are called to seek

His blessing in prayer, in studying His word in fellowship and in meetings. Our program connects addicts with God, and they are delivered from drugs.

I warn parents to keep from drinking or selling alcohol in front of their children. These young minds can easily get affected. I teach the youngest people in my seminars to avoid even the first puff of a cigarette. "Abusing drugs and smoking can wreck your life," I warn young children. Prevention is a better option than a cure, so I am now going to schools, colleges, and universities to bring awareness to students. So far, I have visited several primary schools, secondary schools, and colleges. Drug peddlers peddle drugs and influence students to use them. They say that students are a soft target. Having once been a drug addict myself when I was younger, it is now my duty as a pastor to make sure that I reach students. They quickly open up when I reach out to them.

I believe that my campaign will empower the young and help them to keep away from this evil behavior before they perish. Their choice is to repent or perish. I'm helping even those who are in the experimental stage to get away from it. The addicts are receiving healing in our churches and in our rehabilitation centers, where we are using the Bible as a tool for total healing. Victims are delivered from all bondage, sins, and addictions.

During school holidays, I travel much of the time to reach students. I teach them the symptoms and signs of drug abuse and addictions. I help parents not to remain in denial when they notice that their children are abusing drugs and instead face the challenge and bring those victims to our rehabilitation program. God bless you!

Chapter 8

BE A JOB CREATOR.

I'M LOOKING FOR INDIVIDUALS and organizations to partner with us in our vision of empowering the youth to do business. I'm overwhelmed with gratitude when I see the youth making money in their own businesses after attending my empowering seminars. I'm encouraged by their initial success, for many have decided to move on with what the vision is: to empower them.

All facilitators focus on the initial stages of writing credible business plans. We teach them how to source financing. One of the biggest impediments for starting up a business is having an incoherent plan.

As a pastor, I teach on how to rely on God's help to start a business. You must start by receiving Jesus Christ as your personal savior and have a relationship with God. If you desire to be led by God in whatever you do, you must draw on His power. You will fail in whatever you do if you ignore His power and direction in spite of your skills, experience, connections, or resources.

You must develop an increasing sense of His existence and dependence on Him. But even though you trust upon Him, you can't just sit on the sidelines expecting Him to do everything for you. You must work with your own hands step by step through faith and follow His instructions. Then you can trust Him for the results. God-sufficiency should become your goal, not self-sufficiency. Don't be tempted to do things by yourself in your own strength because you will regret it.

"This is why I do believe that my help comes from the Lord" (Psalm 121:2). God has promised to help me in every situation. My success or victory is assured if I trust and depend on God in my work. I have to confess that I'm depending on God to help me in my life. God is committed to fulfilling His plans for my life.

God created us so that we can do the good things he planned for us to do (Ephesians 2:10). Don't do things your way. Do things God's way, and success will be assured. May God work through you and open a door before you as you obey and do what He has put in your heart to do. The moment you believe in Him; He will give you power to do His will in your life.

Each day, continue depending on God to direct you in your work. Over and over again, He will keep His eyes on you, so promise to give Him His portion of tithes and offerings. Remember that, "It's God who gives you power to get wealth" (Deuteronomy 7:18). Don't ever forget God's word in your life. Once you understand His word, walking with Him will take on a whole new meaning. You will realize that His customized plan for your life is the only plan for your life as in the only plan that will ever satisfy you and make you succeed in your work.

To reach many youths with my empowering teachings, I'm using the Internet and social media. I'm soon starting a center where young people can collect information and other written materials that can empower, equip, and enable them to access benefits from information and communications technology (ICT) affordably. I'm calling it, "The Internet Hub," and I will use it to spread the benefits of youth empowerment in all counties and beyond. You can join us and support the youth to help them start small businesses.

Another important thing I'm teaching the youth is learning to be content. The Bible says, "A man must be content to receive the gift given to him from Heaven" (John 3:37).

We as a church are trying to expand our vision models to ensure that women play a greater role in the economy. Our recent survey revealed that women empowerment is more than an issue for gender equality. As a church, we are working hard to ensure that women are empowered economically, because we do believe that when women participate in the economy, everyone benefits. Women who do business or earn an income are powerful agents of development.

We are helping women to invest in health education and the well-being of their families. We empowering women by trying to remove economic growth barriers in their lives. Barriers, socially, legally, culturally, and politically, could hinder economic progress. We encourage women by telling them that they are drivers of economic growth in the villages, towns, cities, counties, and across the world.

The church has a pivotal role to play in this regard by empowering women to participate in business and the economy. Women should be empowered to start small enterprises in our country. Women have a significant impact on individuals, communities, and economies. That's why we are empowering women to transform communities.

We have noticed that some companies are empowering women retailers, producers, suppliers, and distributors. For example, Equity Bank and other banks are empowering women to start small businesses. They are also empowering the youth to do the same. They are reaching them through seminars and workshops.

Safaricom is championing an initiative to diversify its supplier database as well as build capacity for women-owned businesses. Their goal is to increase spending on women businesses partnering with Safaricom. The vision of those businesses is to entrench inclusive procurement practices within Safaricom. The ultimate mission is to grow the capacity of Kenyan women business owners to be market-ready to access competitive local and global supply chains.

Safaricom is partnering with women in business initiatives. Through partnering, they have increased the number of women vendors. As part of capacity-building, Safaricom is training partners and has held various workshops for women-owned businesses.

Safaricom intends to organize more of these workshops in all counties.

Through these workshops and seminars, Safaricom is hoping to reach out to more women in business. Other big and small companies should emulate Safaricom or Equity Bank in inspiring many women to do business even from the remotest parts of our country.

As a church, we are willing to join hands with such companies, NGOs, and well-wishers in empowering women to actualize their true potential. I would strongly urge other companies and the private sector as a whole to play a more visible role in empowering women to start businesses.

In a nutshell, women empowerment is a powerful tool with which to forge economic prosperity for all. May God help and bless all those companies that are empowering women to start businesses. May these companies perform better in terms of a growing market share and generate more in terms of profits. God bless Safaricom, Equity Bank, and other companies that are empowering women and the youth.

When my son did his Kenya Certificate of Secondary Education in the year 2016, I encouraged him to start farming for money (agribusiness). He started farming a one-acre plot by planting maize. After the harvest, he was able to buy a very expensive smartphone and other important items in his own house. He applied what he had learned in my seminars about money management. The next year, he planted maize in a bigger portion of land, and he expected a big harvest.

"Young man, I want you to know that God has promised in His word to bless the work of your hands. What are you doing now so that God can bless you?"

Robert was another young man in my church in Githurai 45, Nairobi, who benefited from my seminars on youth empowerment.

I personally witnessed the works of this hardworking young man in academic and even social work in the community. Even as he pursued his Bachelor of Commerce in Egerton University, he took up various responsibilities and helped many youths to succeed in life. He was a figure of transformation in the area.

One of the activities Robert spearheaded was garbage collection, something most of his peers ostracized. The youth were making money by serving the community. People in the area respected him very much.

Robert was appointed as the chairman of one of the youth groups, a community-based organization (CBO), which had more than thirty members.

Robert was also involved in other church projects, like preaching the gospel to the lost, building churches, visiting the sick in the hospital, and helping orphans and widows. He received many awards on different platforms for his outstanding performance in transforming the lives of the youth. He promoted the lives of the underserved youth to a higher level. Many youths were changed and transformed from drug addiction and fornication.

Robert is outspoken and perceives things in different perspectives. He never rests until he has achieved a goal or objective. He is very sharp and tactical in his approaches. He helped me to hold youth seminars and to have conventional talks with teens. The church and the community appreciated the good work of this young man. It is my prayer that many young people will emulate him. He is a role model in the community.

In my financial management seminars, I have tips on how you can survive tough financial times. I focus on better money management strategies that can make everybody start a small business instead of complaining that there is no employment. I cover many topics that can make you succeed in life. We talk openly about lifestyles and how to accept reality or the status quo. I motivate the youth on why and how to start a small business with only what they have. I encourage the youth, telling them, "You are a product of your own thoughts." They can therefore plan to succeed or plan to fail. You are a product of your own good choices or bad choices. You will become what you think you are.

There is the power of the beliefs in financial matters. Are you held hostage by your bad beliefs on finances or will you fight to overcome such trouble? Some young people think they should have money all the time; this makes them continue to borrow money without a clear set of goals for it. Others believe that what they have is not enough to start a small business, so they are held hostage by what they don't have. This is a big setback to any business.

The best time to start a small business is now. Waiting for the best time and larger sums of money to begin a small business with will make you a slave. Thinking of getting wealth quickly without working hard to save and invest is dangerous because "easy come, easy go."

We are teaching the youth simple ways to save and invest in a small business that can lead to great wealth progressively step by step. Retrogressive beliefs are making many youths slaves, and they became an impediment to financial freedom. We are warning the youth in our seminars to be aware of such destructive beliefs and avoid them like a plague in order to make financial milestones.

Many youths have been asking me in the seminars about how to start a business. You must know what product or service you want to offer to the community. You must also have in mind of how you want to go about it.

I give the youth important tips on how to start a business. There is nothing that jump-starts any business more than commitment. Are you committed to starting a small business? Your business may look very good on paper, but in the real world, if you don't perform the physical act of starting what you have projected, you will fail. Therefore, consider your commitment first and then start what you have planned to do.

Accept that you have to be continually learning as you sell and chat with your customers. That's to say that if you have planned to sell secondhand shoes, you will learn as you start what your customers really want. Be prepared to act quickly to meet your customers' needs. Otherwise, you will fail. If you want to succeed in any business, forget your former identity and instead adopt your new identity. If you have a degree and are now selling secondhand shoes, don't assume your customers are interested in your degree. They wouldn't care if you got a degree or not. All they'd want is someone who can sell them the type of shoes they are looking for. Forget your titles and/or your previous education and just jump right into your new business verve and enthusiasm, as this will attract your customers.

Don't ever limit your customers. Make them feel like they're the closest people in your life. Forget your former status and your friends, teachers, and schoolmates and just concentrate on your business. Put yourself out there and make sure nobody stands in between. Remember that no business will come looking for you (even if you believe you'll have the world's best products or services). You'll have to look for one.

Businesses do not thrive when in disorder. You must be a very disciplined and organized person. Always be working and planning about your business every day. Have at least a chair and a table where you can be sitting for hours planning out your business alone. Keep all the proper records of cash in and cash out. If you don't treat your business seriously, it will not produce serious results. Sit there and make phone calls, send proposals out, and update your business on your social media pages. Make a list of all your possible networks and contacts, call your potential suppliers, etc.

All success ventures are the results of business owners' consistent actions. Make your business unique. Challenge yourself to do something that will grow or improve your business. When your business is new, it is better to be prepared for how you will serve more customers, because preparation means opportunity. Find time daily to do these important tasks. It will create much needed discipline and give you a sense of progression. These small steps can make a difference in your life as a businessperson.

Remember. "Just start!" You will make it! I have helped many youths to learn how to create jobs instead of seeking for employment. Many of our youths are making a lot of money by creating content in the social media. I love their slogan, "Jitume" which means that you can, send yourself to be our own boss instead of waiting to be employed.

Chapter 9

TRANSFORMING THE YOUTH IN AFRICA

AS A FULL-TIME PASTOR, I am delighted to say that I'm making an impact in delivering the youths from drug abuse and sexual immorality. Former addicts are becoming sober Christians. After transforming the youths, I teach them how they can start making money by using every available means.

Making money is very crucial for survival these days. I tell them that no matter how you get money, it's important to know how you will spend it wisely and how you can save some of it for the future.

The Bible says, "Money answers everything" (Ecclesiastes 10:19). That's why I tell the youths they must try to make money on their own, which will help them to answer all questions in life. Without making money, they will feel hopeless and useless in life. Money will help you to solve your financial obligations and problems. I encourage the youth to stop depending on their parents after school and instead start simple jobs to make their own money. God has promised to bless the work of your hands. So, if you don't work, God will not bless you.

I advise the youth to stop blaming other people and even the government and instead start looking for something they can do to improve the standard of their life. I'm leading the youth in the right ways of making money so that they can improve the standard of their life. All those young people who are following the righteousness are becoming successful in their lives. Keep my words and start doing something to make money. God will lead you into overflowing blessings in your life as a reward.

Learn from the ant, you idle youths. Consider its ways. It works hard without having any chief officer or ruler. It prepares its food in summer and gathers its harvest in time. I speak about the ant in my youth seminars. (Read Proverbs 6:6–8)

Question: How long will you be sitting there idle complaining about your parents and the government? When you wake very late from your sleep and come asking for tea or food that you did not work for? Your little sleep or little slumber will lead you to poverty, you vagabond. Your needs and bills will chase you like an arrow from the enemy.

My words of advice to the youths is to have light in their lives. My reproofs will discipline them and help them to consider how they are living their lives. Stop complaining and do something to improve your life. I have my own adage: "It's better to light a candle than curse darkness with bitterness." Are you good at weeping, begging, and complaining? God wants you to declare a thing and start establishing it. Then He has promised to back that thing you have started. "You will decide on a matter, and it will be established for you, and light will shine upon your way" (Job 22:28).

Wherever you are and wherever you go, God's blessings will follow you. God has promised to bless you in the village and in the city (Deuteronomy 28:1–2). If you don't work with your hands, you will receive no blessings, for there are no blessings for idlers. Depend on God, and he will lead you down the right path in life. He will bless the work of your hands. Jesus warned, "Take head and beware of covetousness, for one's life does not consist in the abundance of the things he possesses" (Luke 12:15).

Don't admire other people's blessings or possessions; work to get your own. The Bible warns, "He who loves money or loves wealth will not be satisfied with money, nor will he gain; this is vanity" (Ecclesiastes 5:10).

Making money is not evil, but the love of money is the root of evil. I teach the youth how to get money in a godly way. Godliness with contentment is great gain.

The Bible says, "You brought nothing out, but all those who desire to be rich quickly will fall into temptation, which could lead them into snare...for the love of money is the root of all kinds of evil" (1 Timothy 6:10).

I know that God lives because when His power moved my life, I was transformed from a drug addict into a gospel messenger. He is the reason I now preach the gospel in this hurting world. And I am not ashamed of the gospel. It is the power of God to give salvation to everyone who believes (Rom 1:16). I am not ashamed to preach about Jesus Christ because He is the one who has the power to save, heal, and deliver sinners from sins, bondage, and addictions.

I preach in season and out of season. I preach the gospel to the youth, which is able to heal their troubled and hurting lives. I am telling the youth to awaken rise and shine, for the light of the gospel has come. I'm encouraging them to love Christ. This is my finest time in history to rescue the youth from the powers of the devil before it's too late. God has given me the favor and grace to minister hope in the lives of many hopeless youths. God is doing a new thing in Africa.

I am teaching the holistic gospel to its body, soul, and mind. I am playing the central role in fostering sound teachings in morals and Biblical values in order to fight drug abuse and the deadly pandemics of HIV that are killing our people. I am teaching the youth the dangers of premarital sex. I am working very hard to reach as many youths as I can before they perish.

In order to succeed in your work, you must involve God with it. For the vision and/or goal you have for your business, be prepared to take risks and pay the price of what will happen in your business. You must be prepared to overcome trials, temptations, challenges, barriers, or hindrances in your business.

Trust God and have confidence in yourself. Ask advice from qualified financial managers or Equity Bank. It is true that as a preacher of the gospel, I am responsible for using the specific gift given to me, and this includes showing practical love to the hopeless youths who are suffering from drug addiction in this world.

I have established that there are significant relationships made in preaching this gospel and helping the hopeless youth succeed in small-scale-businesses. The youth of today need a social-generating programs and small loan schemes. I am helping them with basic training on how to start and manage a successful business.

My seminars are a source of breaking the cycle of poverty and joblessness in the youth. Many youths are experiencing a breakthrough in their lives after our breakthrough seminars in the villages. I am following the steps of Jesus Christ to reach out to the silent suffering youth. We are rescuing them from drug addictions, sexual immorality, poverty, and joblessness. In my attempt to be very effective in reaching the youth for Christ, we registered "Stay Up Rehabilitation Community-Based Organization." A Seminar in Entrepreneurship.

Since 2005, the church has been participating in several workshops and seminars. We have learnt about how to do many things, like zero-grazing, poultry-keeping, beekeeping, and agribusiness. We learn on socioeconomic issues, the marketing of farm produce, and environment management.

On May 14, 2011, at Kanorero Primary School in the Kiambogo location of Gilgil, I participated in a seminar that was conducted by the Equity Bank Gilgil branch. The seminar was facilitated by George Njenga from Equity Bank. We started the seminar with prayers at

10 AM. Equity Bank's intention was to enrich and empower the participants in financial management in their homes, farms, and businesses. Equity Bank's desire was to take its services to the local people in the villages of the rural areas.

The seminar focused on the main areas of financial management issues concerning small-scale-business owners and small-scale farmers. They were doing capacity-building in the villages in the area. All participants remained intact in all sessions as Mr. Kingori steered the high spirit and cohesion of all participants. There were several reasons behind these seminars. The main one being Equity Bank development approaches in the forgotten rural areas. The bank is trying to improve the livelihood of small-scale farmers and business people. It is also enhancing on food security for all households in the villages.

The seminar was divided into six main topics, namely: budget, expenditure, marketing, savings, loans, and bank services.

Budget

I teach participants the importance of having a budget at home, in your farm, and in your business. A facilitator stressed the importance of focusing on your vision, dreams, and goals, as well as being realistic and having the right timing in your home, farm, and businesses. He taught us two types of goals:

1. Long-term goals like constructing a permanent building and educating your children to the highest levels.
2. Short-term goals like buying clothes for the family and buying food.

Spendthrift

Many people in the rural areas use much of their money for drinking the illicit brews like chang'aa. I teach them how to use their money wisely and how to identify their needs. I advise them to live within their means and buy for their families' things that they can afford; pay school fees, travel where necessary, pay bills, and at least save something.

Marketing

I advised small-scale farmers to plant their seeds in the right time so as to increase their harvests. He told them to prepare the seeds before the sowing season. I explained to them the danger of planting during the wrong season.

I advise farmers not to sell their produce immediately after harvest at a throw-away price but instead wait patiently until the price is higher. This is called "value addition."

For example, one bag of maize would sell at Ksh. 2,800 (+/-500) during the harvest season, but if you can wait for about five to six months, the same bag will sell at Ksh. 4000 (+/-500). Another example is that a bag of beans would sell at Ksh. 4,000 (+/-500) during harvest season, and after six months the same bag would sell at Ksh. 6,000 (+/-500). This is what, as a facilitator, I called "value addition." The seminar has helped us to learn very valuable lessons on capacity-building, and it promotes our effects in production, value addition, and marketing.

Savings

Some of the good reasons for saving money in the bank. We are to save for our long-term goals, like building, business, education, retirement, and emergencies. I advised the participants on how to save in the form of assets and investments. We are to save for some unexpected future events in our lives.

Saving is hard work, and therefore we are to spend less than we earn so that we are to spare some money to save. He told us to choose the right institutions to save our money in like banks, Sacco's, CBOs, and companies with a share of other institutions.

He warned us to be careful when saving because some banks and institutions charge large amounts of money in ledger fees and higher interests. He warned us not to invest in pyramid schemes. He also taught us about how to buy shares in companies and how to save where our money can be easily accessed when it is required.

Loans

Equity Bank has made it very easy for its members to get loans. As an example, there is the "Kilimo" loan, which is offered to the youth through a loan known as "Vukisha" at 8% interest rate. I had made it for us churches to save, for example, by opening a Neema Account.

The youth are required to be registered with the ministry of youth to qualify for a loan. Another condition for the youth is that you must at least be saving 100 shillings per week. The amount you save will be multiplied by five when you are applying for a loan. I urge Christians to give God tithes and offerings and to save through a Neema Account for churches.

There is money that is given to business people, and for women there is the "Fanikisha Wamama" fund. This loan is given to women only. It has lifted many hopeless lives of women in the country. Women are using these loans to improve their livelihood. Other services include buying Yamaha motorbikes and water tanks, as well as doing farming or managing greenhouses. Ask for these services in the nearest bank. Loans are given to boost your business. The best reason to apply for a loan is for investment.

Banking Services

I like Equity Bank because it has extended all of its services to rural areas through its agents. They have chosen people in a given area to serve customers who used to have to travel long distances to reach the nearest branch of Equity Bank. Through their agents you can save, withdraw, and check your balance. Some agents are offering automated teller machine (ATM) services. The bank offers the "Jinjenge" account, the fixed deposit account, and the Super Junior accounts for your children. To open this junior account, you need a birth certificate for your children.

The bank has insurance coverage; for environment issues as well as education sponsorship for needy students. For all those customers who have friends or relatives who can send them money from abroad, the bank has services like RTGS, SWIFT, Western Union, and Money Gram. The participants were grateful for all their questions concerning financial management being answered. I kept them in expectancy until the seminar ended without their knowledge.

As we were going home from the venue of the seminar, our hearts were on fire. We improved our lives in businesses and in farming. The seminar helped us because we were willing to change. We were driven by our patience, openness, and willingness to change our financial management. We are willing to change, and we were ready for new challenges as we began focusing on establishing a development plan for the ultimate welfare of our families.

Our CBO has been a very instrumental organization with its financial management seminars in the rural areas. It has brought together different tribes to collaborate in self-help groups and CBOs to share their financial management skills. Equity is an institution of excellence because it's helping its members in the rural areas in identifying priorities when applying for a loan. It was after these financial management seminars that applying for our loans could be easily made possible.

I encourage the youth groups to go to Equity Bank for loans and opening bank accounts. Many have gained much in the seminar, mostly in the process of priority setting. The topics have helped many churches embrace this idea of saving with Equity Bank.

I am very transparent, holistic, and realistic. In fact, let me say that this was the only seminar that I participated in where the real stakeholders, the small-scale business people and farmers, were involved as participants and were allowed to ask questions freely.

I used a coherent participation approach like Equity Bank by involving the rural communities in solving their financial management problems. The bank is reaching the rural folk using their modern technologies and new ideas of how to handle finances.

Equity has good policies of emphasizing closer cooperation with the rural folk. It has made simple villagers into self-help groups and CBOs in the rural areas to build more confidence with this caring bank.

The most visible contribution of Equity Bank is improving the livelihoods of the hopeless youth, women, and small-scale business people and farmers in the rural areas. Let me thank the Equity Bank management for their willingness to reach the unreached rural folk. The seminar equipped and promoted many in our area. Business people improved their businesses and churches improved their financial management skills.

This is why I am targeting the youth in empowerment projects in our area. I tell the youths that these days, going to school and getting a university education does not guarantee you a job. I am encouraging the youths to come to us and experience new farming methods and learn how to start a small-scale business. We are learning about job creation and we are emphasizing on monitoring and evaluation as major parts in both business and farm management.

As a young person, remember that the Bible says, "Money answers everything" (Ecclesiastes 10:19). Join our financial education group, and you will learn more about management. Many youths in our group have improved after using financial knowledge they have learnt in our organization.

We are joining Equity Bank in transforming Africa by empowering the youth and encouraging them to engage in entrepreneurship. My message to the youth is, "Stop complaining and instead start working." I was happy to receive a certificate of participation after completing my training in financial education on November 18, 2011, in the Gilgil Town. The certificate was signed by Dr. James Mwangi, the MBS chairman, the Equity Group Foundation, Reepa Roy the president and CEO, and the Master Card Foundation. The training changed our youth from complaining to working with their own hands. The youth in my church expressed inexpressible joy.

I would kindly request all other banking institutions to emulate Equity Bank in educating the community on financial management skills. The youth have changed from idlers to self-employed people. Long live Equity Bank. God bless the founders for their vision of transforming the youth and women in Africa. The Gospel Messengers Church is working hard to transform the youth in Kenya.

We are transforming drug addicts into successful Christian business people. We are trying to raise a new generation of our youth who will be the future leaders. I am called by God in my ministry to transform the youth, and I am targeting youth entrepreneurship projects. My own inborn compassion to transform the youth is propelled by my strong faith in Jesus Christ. I have a dream of giving hope to the hopeless in Africa.

In my spirit, I feel that I want to achieve even more, and my aspiration is to respond quickly to the needs of the youths. I do believe that together with all stakeholders we are going to make great strides in transforming the youth in Africa. Africa is in my heart and the world is in my mind. Africa, awake! Arise! And shine! Your light has come!

About the Author

PETER. N. MUYA HAS worked with Full Gospel Church and Redeemed Gospel Church, before starting his own ministry, Gospel Messengers Church.

He was born in 1955 in Nyonjoro farm, Lanet, Nakuru County. He has a Bachelor's degree in ministry, an associate's degree in biblical studies and Counseling.

He is married to Mary Muya, and they have three children who are adults working in different parts of our country.

He is the founder and the Bishop of Gospel Messengers Church in East Africa.

About Us

Gospel Messengers Church is a nonprofit dedicated to transforming lives in Kenya's most marginalized communities. Committed to eradicating female genital mutilation (FGM), poverty, and illiteracy, the organization builds schools, provides clean water through boreholes, and empowers communities through education and sustainable development.

By addressing social injustices and uplifting vulnerable populations, Gospel Messengers Church fosters hope and opportunity for the less fortunate.

You can Donate via M-Pesa Pay Bill no: 880100 a/c: 5146870014.

You can also use PayPal email: messengergospel13@gmail.com

THESE ARE OUR BANK DETAILS FOR INTERNATIONAL MONEY TRANSFERS.

Bank Name	NCBA BANK KENYA PLC
Branch Name	NAKURU
Branch Code	000 (for any branch)
Bank Full Address	P.O. BOX 44599–00100, NAIROBI – KENYA
Bank Account Name	GOSPEL MESSENGER CHURCH
Bank Code	07
Bank Account Number	5146870014
SWIFT /BIC Code	CBAFKENX

Also by Peter N Muya

Kill Me Not
Love Without Lust
Do Not Weep
Death From Illicit Brew
Hope For Survival
I Shall Not Die
Never Lose Hope

Watch for more at https://www.gospelmessengerschurch.com.

www.ingramcontent.com/pod-product-compliance
Lightning Source LLC
Chambersburg PA
CBHW071345150726
47997CB00002B/862